DOCTRINE

& COVENANTS

2021 STUDY SCHEDULE

December 28 - January 3	Doctrine and Covenants 1
January 4 - 10	Joseph Smith-History 1:1-26
January 11 - 17	Doctrine and Covenants 2; Joseph Smith-History 1:27–65
January 18 - 24	Doctrine and Covenants 3–5
January 25 - 31	Doctrine and Covenants 6–9
February 1 - 7	Doctrine and Covenants 10–11
February 8 - 14	Doctrine and Covenants 12–13; Joseph Smith-History 1:66–75
February 15 - 21	Doctrine and Covenants 14–17
February 22 - 28	Doctrine and Covenants 18–19
March 1 - 7	Doctrine and Covenants 20–22
March 8 - 14	Doctrine and Covenants 23–26
March 15 - 21	Doctrine and Covenants 27–28
March 22 - 28	Doctrine and Covenants 29
March 29 - April 4	Easter
April 5 - 11	Doctrine and Covenants 30–36
April 12 - 18	Doctrine and Covenants 37–40
April 19 - 25	Doctrine and Covenants 41–44
April 26 - May 2	Doctrine and Covenants 45
May 3 - 9	Doctrine and Covenants 46–48
May 10 - 16	Doctrine and Covenants 49–50
May 17 - 23	Doctrine and Covenants 51–57
May 24 - 30	Doctrine and Covenants 58–59
May 31 - June 6	Doctrine and Covenants 60–62
June 7 - 13	Doctrine and Covenants 63
June 14 - 20	Doctrine and Covenants 64–66
June 21 - 27	Doctrine and Covenants 67–70
June 28 - July 4	Doctrine and Covenants 71–75
July 5 - 11	Doctrine and Covenants 76
July 12 - 18	Doctrine and Covenants 77–80
July 19 - 25	Doctrine and Covenants 81–83
July 26 - August 1	Doctrine and Covenants 84
August 2 - 8	Doctrine and Covenants 85–87
August 9 - 15	Doctrine and Covenants 88
August 16 - 22	Doctrine and Covenants 89–92
August 23 - 29	Doctrine and Covenants 93
August 30 - September 5	Doctrine and Covenants 94–97
September 6 - 12	Doctrine and Covenants 98–101
September 13 - 19	Doctrine and Covenants 102–105
September 20 - 26	Doctrine and Covenants 106–108
September 27 - October 3	Doctrine and Covenants 109–110
October 4 - 10	Doctrine and Covenants 111–114
October 11 - 17	Doctrine and Covenants 115–120
October 18 - 24	Doctrine and Covenants 121–123
October 25 - 31	Doctrine and Covenants 124
November 1 - 7	Doctrine and Covenants 125–128
November 8 - 14	Doctrine and Covenants 129–132
November 15 - 21	Doctrine and Covenants 133–134
November 22 - 28	Doctrine and Covenants 135–136
November 29 - December 5	Doctrine and Covenants 137–138
December 6 - 12	The Articles of Faith and Official Declarations 1 and 2
December 13 - 19	The Family: A Proclamation to the World
December 20-26	Christmas
December 27 - January 2	Old Testament 2022

SKU# B047

DOCTRINE & COVENANTS

STUDY BOOK

TABLE OF CONTENTS

TABLE OF CONTENTS

DM = Seminary Doctrinal Mastery Scripture

SAMPLE PAGE

Title
Once you have studied the section, decide on a title that properly explains that section. Write your title at the top.

What was happening:
Write the background for the section. This can be found in the section heading. At times we have provided an explanation for you if some more detail would help you understand the purpose behind the revelation. When you understand the reason the revelation was given, you can often discover additional doctrines and principles.

Section

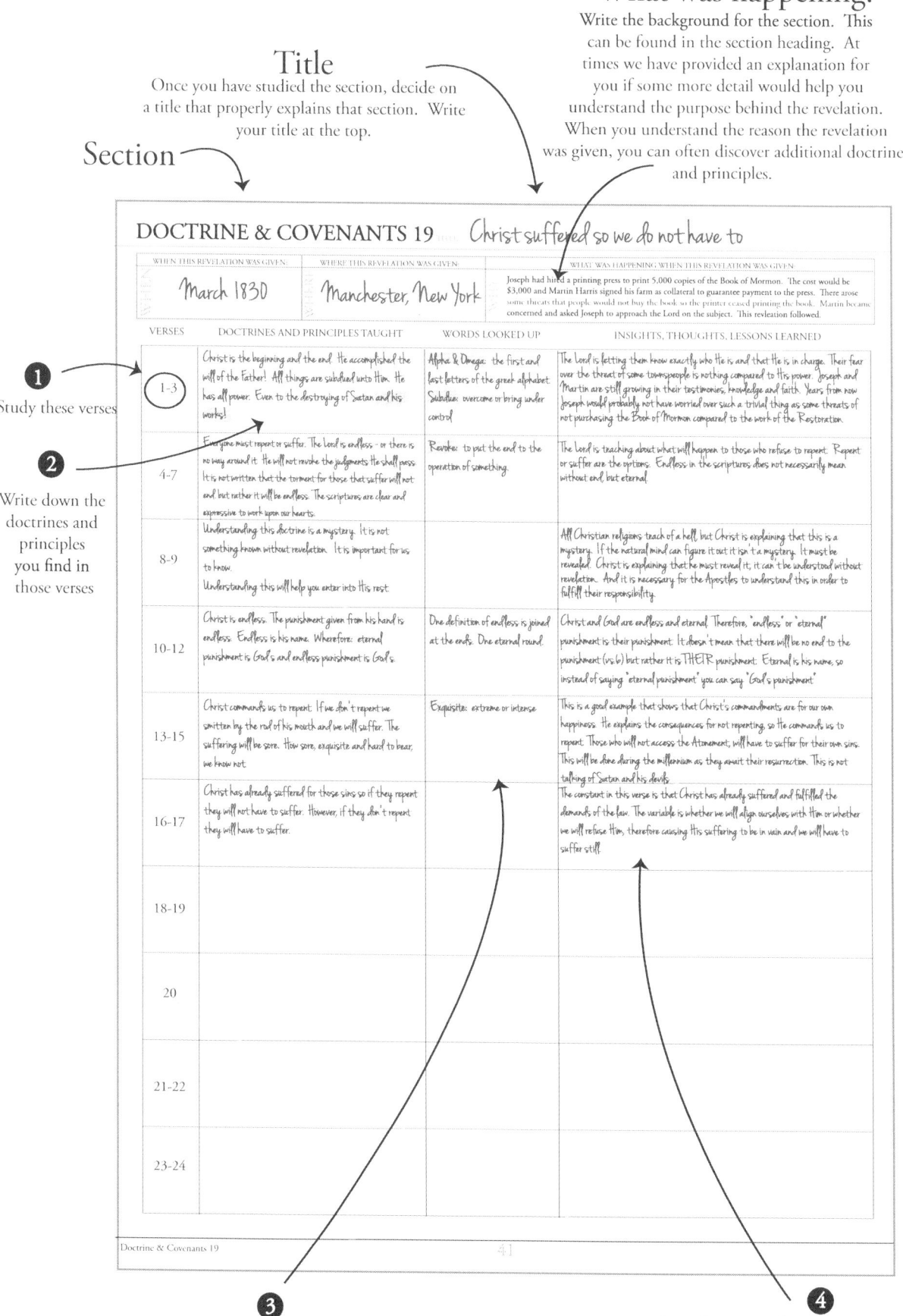

DOCTRINE & COVENANTS 19 — Christ suffered so we do not have to

WHEN THIS REVELATION WAS GIVEN:	WHERE THIS REVELATION WAS GIVEN:	WHAT WAS HAPPENING WHEN THIS REVELATION WAS GIVEN:
March 1830	Manchester, New York	Joseph had hired a printing press to print 5,000 copies of the Book of Mormon. The cost would be $3,000 and Martin Harris signed his farm as collateral to guarantee payment to the press. There arose some threats that people would not buy the book so the printer ceased printing the book. Martin became concerned and asked Joseph to approach the Lord on the subject. This revelation followed.

VERSES	DOCTRINES AND PRINCIPLES TAUGHT	WORDS LOOKED UP	INSIGHTS, THOUGHTS, LESSONS LEARNED
1-3	Christ is the beginning and the end. He accomplished the will of the Father! All things are subdued unto Him. He has all power. Even to the destroying of Satan and his works!	Alpha & Omega: the first and last letters of the greek alphabet. Subdue: overcome or bring under control	The Lord is letting them know exactly who He is and that He is in charge. Their fear over the threat of some townspeople is nothing compared to His power. Joseph and Martin are still growing in their testimonies, knowledge and faith. Years from now Joseph would probably not have worried over such a trivial thing as some threats of not purchasing the Book of Mormon compared to the work of the Restoration.
4-7	Everyone must repent or suffer. The Lord is endless - or there is no way around it. He will not revoke the judgments He shall pass. It is not written that the torment for those that suffer will not end, but rather it will be endless. The scriptures are clear and expressive to work upon our hearts.	Revoke: to put the end to the operation of something.	The Lord is teaching about what will happen to those who refuse to repent. Repent or suffer are the options. Endless in the scriptures does not necessarily mean without end, but eternal.
8-9	Understanding this doctrine is a mystery. It is not something known without revelation. It is important for us to know. Understanding this will help you enter into His rest.		All Christian religions teach of a hell, but Christ is explaining that this is a mystery. If the natural mind can figure it out it isn't a mystery. It must be revealed. Christ is explaining that he must reveal it, it can't be understood without revelation. And it is necessary for the Apostles to understand this in order to fulfill their responsibility.
10-12	Christ is endless. The punishment given from his hand is endless. Endless is his name. Wherefore: eternal punishment is God's and endless punishment is God's.	One definition of endless is joined at the ends. One eternal round.	Christ and God are endless and eternal. Therefore, "endless" or "eternal" punishment is their punishment. It doesn't mean that there will be no end to the punishment (vs 6) but rather it is THEIR punishment. Eternal is his name, so instead of saying "eternal punishment" you can say "God's punishment"
13-15	Christ commands us to repent. If we don't repent we smitten by the rod of his mouth and we will suffer. The suffering will be sore. How sore, exquisite and hard to bear, we know not	Exquisite: extreme or intense	This is a good example that shows that Christ's commandments are for our own happiness. He explains the consequences for not repenting, so he commands us to repent. Those who will not access the Atonement, will have to suffer for their own sins. This will be done during the millennium as they await their resurrection. This is not talking of Satan and his devils.
16-17	Christ has already suffered for those sins so if they repent they will not have to suffer. However, if they don't repent they will have to suffer.		The constant in this verse is that Christ has already suffered and fulfilled the demands of the law. The variable is whether we will align ourselves with Him or whether we will refuse Him, therefore causing His suffering to be in vain and we will have to suffer still.
18-19			
20			
21-22			
23-24			

1 Study these verses

2 Write down the doctrines and principles you find in those verses

3 Look up words you do not know or would like more clarity on, and write the definitions.

4 Record your insights, lessons learned, commentary teaching ideas, etc.

SAMPLE PAGE
25 Doctrinal Mastery Study Pages

There are 25 Seminary Doctrinal Mastery Passages pages included in this book. These contain doctrines and principles that provide essential gospel knowledge and strengthen faith. A study page has been dedicated to each Doctrinal Mastery so you can have an in-depth study and ponder these important scriptures.

DOCTRINE & COVENANTS 8:2-3

THE HOLY GHOST SPEAKS TO OUR MINDS AND HEARTS

2 Yea, behold, I will tell you in your mind and in your heart, by the Holy Ghost, which shall come upon you and which shall dwell in your heart.
3 Now, behold, this is the spirit of revelation; behold, this is the spirit by which Moses brought the children of Israel through the Red Sea on dry ground.

DOCTRINE & COVENANTS 8:2-3

"An impression to the mind is very specific.
"Detailed words can be heard or felt and written as though the instruction were being dictated.
"A communication to the heart is a more general impression. The Lord often begins by giving impressions. Where there is a recognition of their importance and they are obeyed, one gains more capacity to receive more detailed instruction to the mind. An impression to the heart, if followed, is fortified by a more specific instruction to the mind" ("Helping Others to Be Spiritually Led" [address to CES religious educators, Aug. 11, 1998], 3–4, LDS.org). **ELDER RICHARD G. SCOTT**

1. Make a list of all of the doctrines and principles you can find in these verses:

2. When Moses arrived at the Red Sea as he led the children of Israel out of Egypt and the Egyptian soldiers came after them, how did Moses think of (and then act upon) separating the waters of the Red Sea and leading the Israelites through the sea?

3. What do you think others might have thought of in that situation? What solutions would come to the average person's mind on how to protect hundreds of thousands of Israelites from the powerful Egyptian army?

4. What can you learn from this? Why is it important for us to understand how to receive revelation?

5. What are some ways the Lord can speak to our minds (as stated in verse 2)?

6. What are some ways the Lord can speak to our hearts (also stated in verse 2)?

7. What do these scriptures teach you about the seminary doctrinal topic: "Acquiring Spiritual Knowledge"?

THE PLAN OF SALVATION

Label this Plan of Salvation and as you study throughout the year, write notes all over this page of things you learn about different parts of the Plan.

UNDERSTANDING THE

Answer these questions using the "Explanatory Introduction"
found in the front of your Doctrine and Covenants.

1. What is the Doctrine and Covenants?

2. What is the purpose of the Doctrine and Covenants?

3. Who can benefit from the messages in the Doctrine and Covenants?

4. Who received most of the revelations in the Doctrine and Covenants?

5. Who received the revelations in the following sections? (Look up the sections and read the section headings)

   136
   138

6. What are the four books in the "standard works of the Church"?

   1- _____   2- _____

   3- _____   4- _____

7. In what way is the Doctrine and Covenants unique from other scripture?

8. What does one "hear" in the Doctrine and Covenants?

9. The work (that is explained and set forth in the Doctrine & Covenants) is in preparation for what?

10. What was Joseph Smith told during the First Vision?

11. What was Joseph Smith told he would do?

12. What are some significant things that Joseph Smith accomplished and received?

13. What happened on April 6, 1830? Why was this day significant?

14. Fill in the blanks:

    "These sacred revelations were received in answer to _____, in times of _____, and came out of _____-_____"
    situations involving real _____."

15. What does one "see" in the revelations?

16. What are 12 examples of doctrines taught in the Doctrine and Covenants?

   1   **5**   **9**

   2   **6**   **10**

   3   **7**   **11**

   4   **8**   **12**

17. What administrative structure is shown forth in the Doctrine and Covenants?

18. What makes this book of great value and of more worth than all of the riches of the earth?

19. Many of the revelations in the Doctrine and Covenants were published in another book. What was that book called, and when and where was it published?

20. When was the Doctrine and Covenants first published?

21. What was attached to the Doctrine and Covenants?

22. After the Doctrine and Covenants was first published, more editions followed. What has been added to those other editions?

23. What was in the 1835 edition that is no longer part of the current edition of the Doctrine and Covenants?

24. Why were they removed?

25. What three documents were added for the first time in this current edition of the Doctrine and Covenants (added in 1981)?

   1

   2

   3

26. What type of corrections have been made in the Doctrine and Covenants?

27. What other features have been added in this latest edition?

* Look up "Chronological Order of Contents" at the beginning of your Doctrine and Covenants and answer the following questions:

   28. How many revelations were received in 1830?

   29. How many revelations were received in the following places:

Manchester, New York	Harmony, Pennsylvania	Fayette, New York	Kirtland, Ohio	Zion, Jackson County, Missouri	By the Missouri River
Hiram, Ohio	Orange, Ohio	Amherst, Ohio	Independence, Missouri	Perrysburg, New York	Fishing River, Missouri
Salem, Massachusetts	Far West, Missouri	Spring Hill, Missouri	Liberty Jail	Nauvoo, Illinois	Ramus, Illinois
Winter Quarters	Salt Lake City, Utah				

4

CHURCH HISTORY TIMELINE
1805-1868

Look up "Chronology of Church History" in the back of your Doctrine and Covenants (just before the maps). Write what is happening on each date on the timeline. As you study the Doctrine and Covenants and Church History, you can come back to this page and add additional information by writing in dates and information in the proper places. You can also add your own family history and personal information (birth, blessing, baptism, etc.) into the timeline.

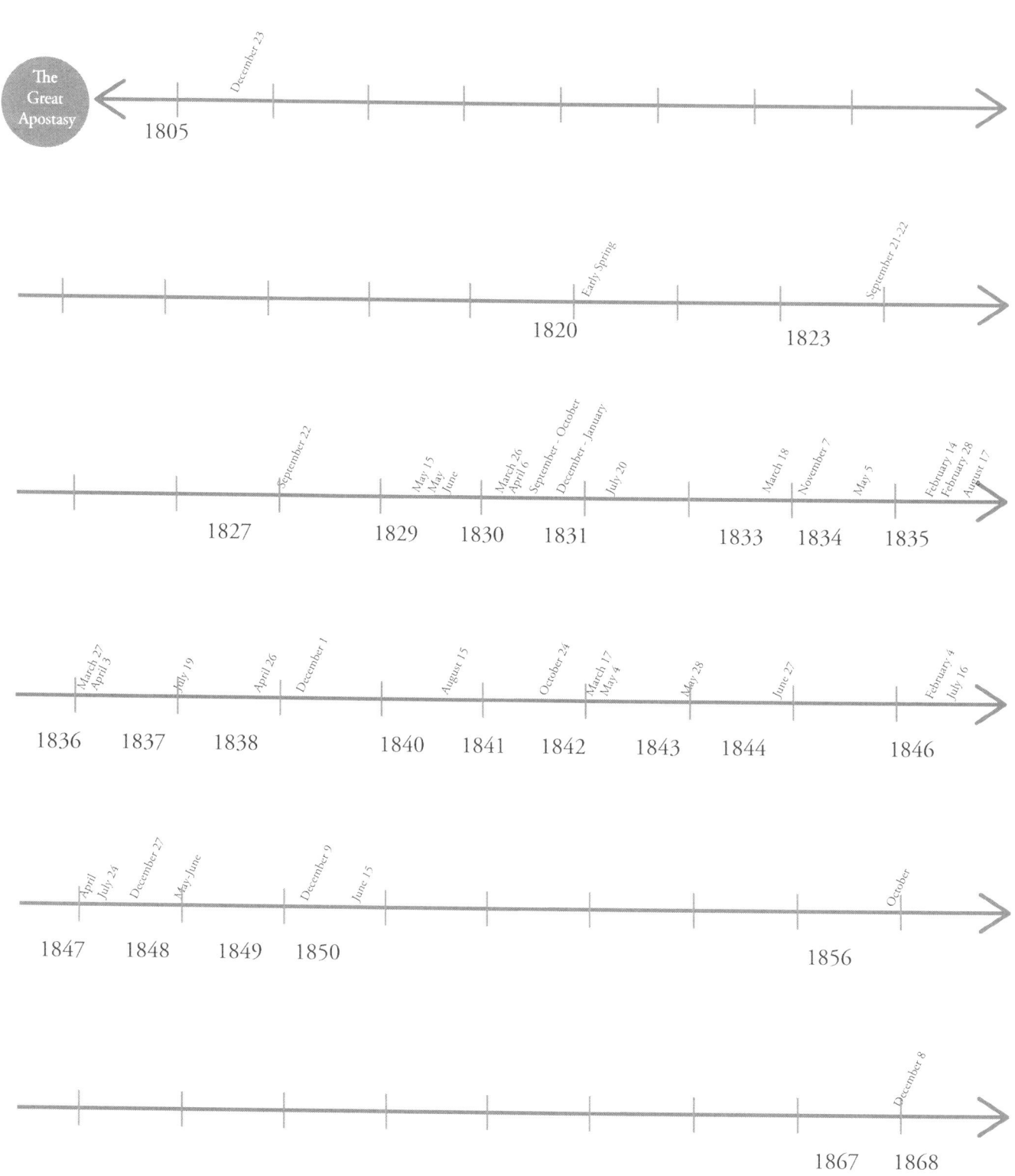

5

CHURCH HISTORY TIMELINE

1869-1934

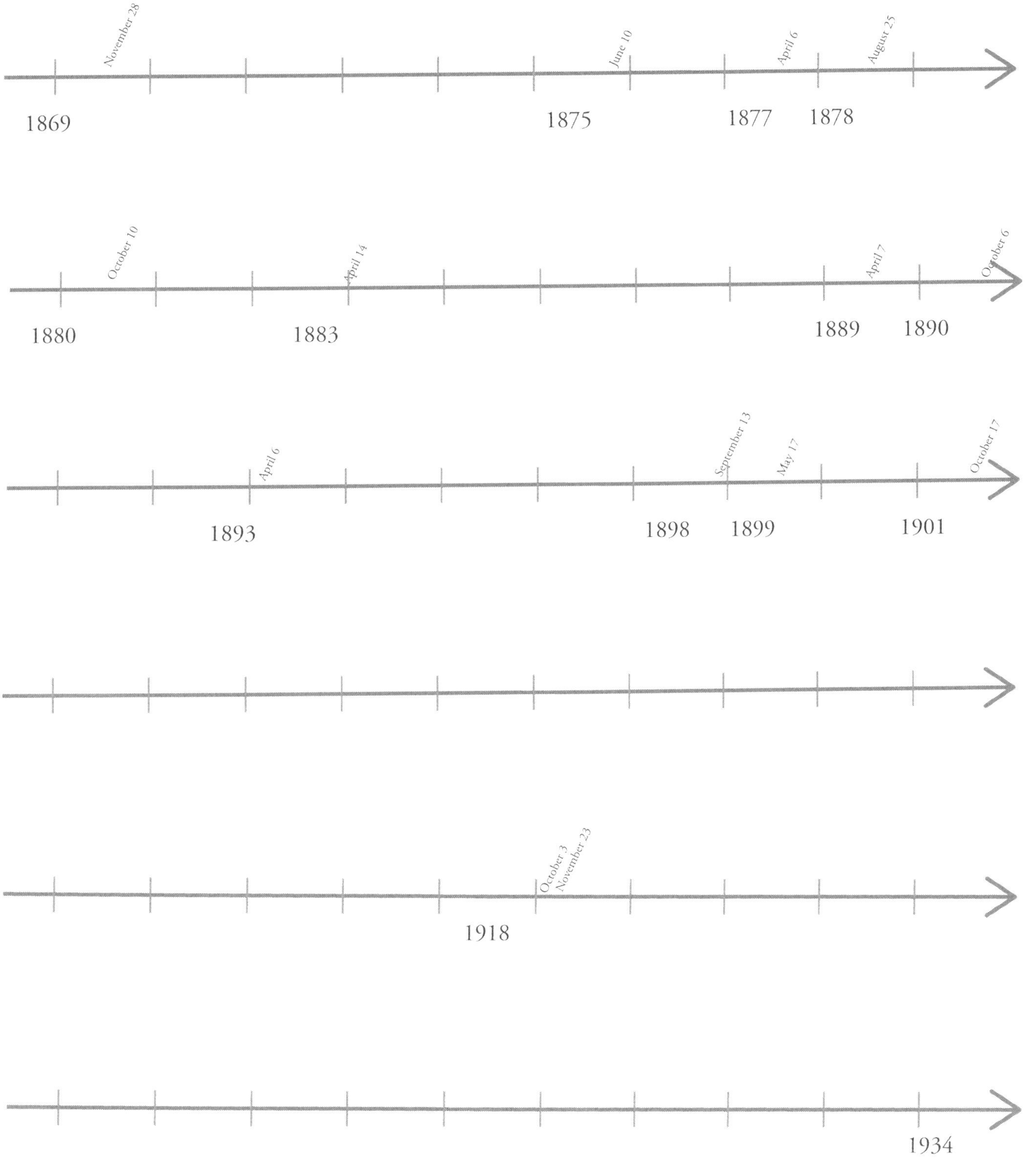

November 28

June 10   April 6   August 25

1869   1875   1877   1878

October 10   April 14   April 7   October 6

1880   1883   1889   1890

April 6   September 13   May 17   October 17

1893   1898   1899   1901

October 3
November 23

1918

1934

CHURCH HISTORY TIMELINE

1935-2000

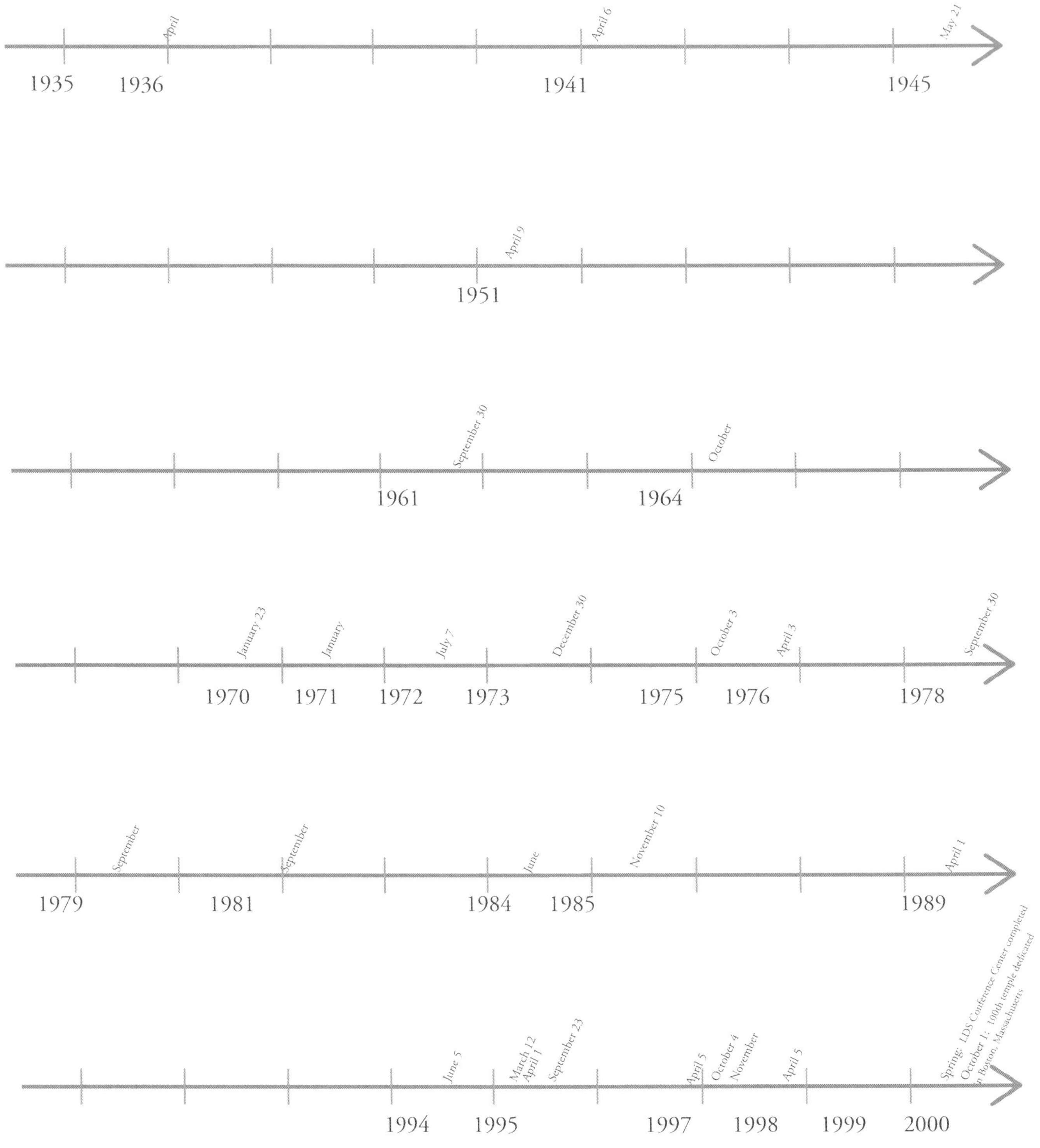

1935 — April — **1936** — April 6 — **1941** — May 21 — **1945**

April 9 — **1951**

September 30 — **1961** — October — **1964**

January 23 — **1970** — January — **1971** — July 7 — **1972** — **1973** — December 30 — **1975** — October 3 — **1976** — April 3 — September 30 — **1978**

September — **1979** — September — **1981** — June — **1984** — November 10 — **1985** — April 1 — **1989**

June 5 — **1994** — March 12 — April 1 — **1995** — September 23 — **1997** — April 5 — October 4 — **1998** — November — **1999** — April 5 — **2000** — Spring: LDS Conference Center completed / October 1: 100th temple dedicated in Boston, Massachusetts

CHURCH HISTORY TIMELINE

2001-2066

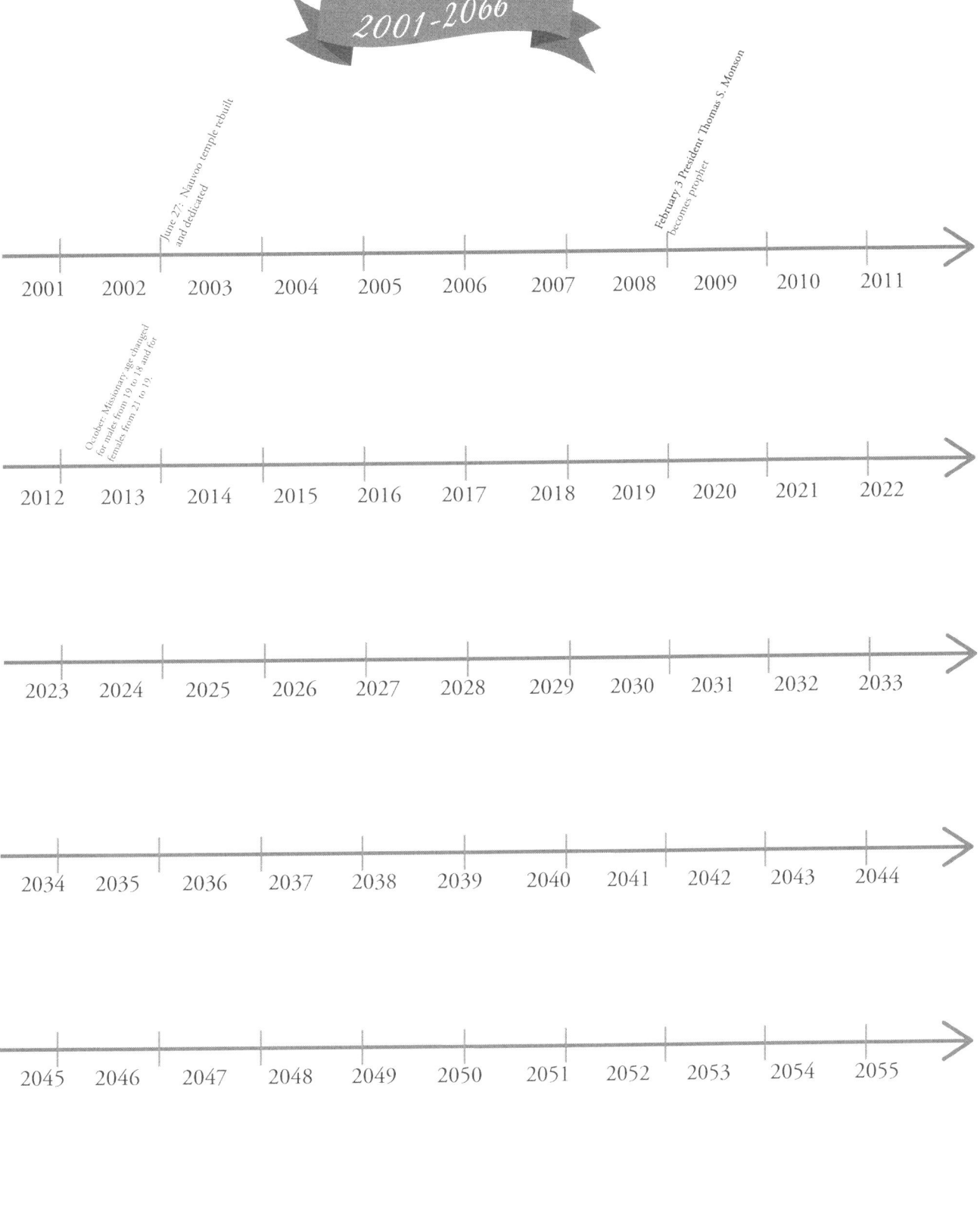

June 27: Nauvoo temple rebuilt and dedicated

February 3 President Thomas S. Monson becomes prophet

2001 2002 2003 2004 2005 2006 2007 2008 2009 2010 2011

October: Missionary age changed for males from 19 to 18 and for females from 21 to 19.

2012 2013 2014 2015 2016 2017 2018 2019 2020 2021 2022

2023 2024 2025 2026 2027 2028 2029 2030 2031 2032 2033

2034 2035 2036 2037 2038 2039 2040 2041 2042 2043 2044

2045 2046 2047 2048 2049 2050 2051 2052 2053 2054 2055

2056 2057 2058 2059 2060 2061 2062 2063 2064 2065 2066

JOSEPH SMITH-HISTORY 1:1-20 TITLE

VERSES	OVERVIEW OF WHAT IS HAPPENING OR BEING TAUGHT	WORDS LOOKED UP	INSIGHTS, THOUGHTS, LESSONS LEARNED, DOCTRINES AND PRINCIPLES FOUND
1-2			
3-4	JOSEPH SMITH'S EARLY LIFE	JOSEPH SMITH'S FAMILY	JOSEPH SMITH SR. — LUCY MACK SMITH
5			
6			
7-8			
9			
10			
11			
12			
13-14			

TITLE:

VERSES	OVERVIEW OF WHAT IS HAPPENING OR BEING TAUGHT	WORDS LOOKED UP	INSIGHTS, THOUGHTS, LESSONS LEARNED, DOCTRINES AND PRINCIPLES FOUND
15			
16			
17			
18			
19			
20			

Lessons

WHAT ARE SOME OF THE MOST IMPORTANT LESSONS YOU CAN LEARN FROM THESE SCRIPTURES?

IN THE FIRST VISION,
GOD CALLED JOSEPH SMITH TO BE A PROPHET

15 After I had retired to the place where I had previously designed to go, having looked around me, and finding myself alone, I kneeled down and began to offer up the desires of my heart to God. I had scarcely done so, when immediately I was seized upon by some power which entirely overcame me, and had such an astonishing influence over me as to bind my tongue so that I could not speak. Thick darkness gathered around me, and it seemed to me for a time as if I were doomed to sudden destruction. 16 But, exerting all my powers to call upon God to deliver me out of the power of this enemy which had seized upon me, and at the very moment when I was ready to sink into despair and abandon myself to destruction—not to an imaginary ruin, but to the power of some actual being from the unseen world, who had such marvelous power as I had never before felt in any being—just at this moment of great alarm, I saw a pillar of light exactly over my head, above the brightness of the sun, which descended gradually until it fell upon me.
17 It no sooner appeared than I found myself delivered from the enemy which held me bound. When the light rested upon me I saw two Personages, whose brightness and glory defy all description, standing above me in the air. One of them spake unto me, calling me by name and said, pointing to the other—This is My Beloved Son. Hear Him!
18 My object in going to inquire of the Lord was to know which of all the sects was right, that I might know which to join. No sooner, therefore, did I get possession of myself, so as to be able to speak, than I asked the Personages who stood above me in the light, which of all the sects was right (for at this time it had never entered into my heart that all were wrong)—and which I should join.
19 I was answered that I must join none of them, for they were all wrong; and the Personage who addressed me said that all their creeds were an abomination in his sight; that those professors were all corrupt; that: "they draw near to me with their lips, but their hearts are far from me, they teach for doctrines the commandments of men, having a form of godliness, but they deny the power thereof."
20 He again forbade me to join with any of them; and many other things did he say unto me, which I cannot write at this time. When I came to myself again, I found myself lying on my back, looking up into heaven. When the light had departed, I had no strength; but soon recovering in some degree, I went home. And as I leaned up to the fireplace, mother inquired what the matter was. I replied, "Never mind, all is well—I am well enough off." I then said to my mother, "I have learned for myself that Presbyterianism is not true." It seems as though the adversary was aware, at a very early period of my life, that I was destined to prove a disturber and an annoyer of his kingdom; else why should the powers of darkness combine against me? Why the opposition and persecution that arose against me, almost in my infancy?

"Our entire case as members of The Church of Jesus Christ of Latter-day Saints rests on the validity of this glorious First Vision. It was the parting of the curtain to open this, the dispensation of the fulness of times. Nothing on which we base our doctrine, nothing we teach, nothing we live by is of greater importance than this initial declaration. I submit that if Joseph Smith talked with God the Father and His Beloved Son, then all else of which he spoke is true. This is the hinge on which turns the gate that leads to the path of salvation and eternal life"

PRESIDENT GORDON B. HINCKLEY
Ensign, Nov. 1998, 71

1. Make a list of 5 doctrines (truths) or principles you can find in these verses.

      1-

      2-

      3-

      4-

      5-

2. Why do you think Satan tried to stop Joseph Smith from praying?

3. What specific things did Joseph Smith learn from the First Vision?

4. What phrase from these verses is the most meaningful to you? Why?

5. What do these scriptures teach you about the seminary doctrinal topic: "The Restoration"?

DOCTRINE & COVENANTS 1:30

THE ONLY TRUE AND LIVING CHURCH

And also those to whom these commandments were given, might have power to lay the foundation of this church, and to bring it forth out of obscurity and out of darkness, the only true and living church upon the face of the whole earth, with which I, the Lord, am well pleased, speaking unto the church collectively and not individually

DOCTRINE & COVENANTS 1:30

"Now this is not to say that the churches, all of them, are without some truth. They have some truth—some of them very much of it. They have a form of godliness. Often the clergy and adherents are not without dedication, and many of them practice remarkably well the virtues of Christianity. They are, nonetheless, incomplete. ...

"The gospel might be likened to the keyboard of a piano—a full keyboard with a selection of keys on which one who is trained can play a variety without limits; a ballad to express love, a march to rally, a melody to soothe, and a hymn to inspire; an endless variety to suit every mood and satisfy every need.

"How shortsighted it is, then, to choose a single key and endlessly tap out the monotony of a single note, or even two or three notes, when the full keyboard of limitless harmony can be played.

"How disappointing when the fullness of the gospel, the whole keyboard, is here upon the earth, that many churches tap on a single key. The note they stress may be essential to a complete harmony of religious experience, but it is, nonetheless, not all there is. It isn't the fullness. ...

"Now we do not say they are wrong so much as we say they are incomplete. The fullness of the gospel has been restored. The power and the authority to act for Him is present with us. The power and the authority of the priesthood rests upon this church.

"... The Church of Jesus Christ of Latter-day Saints is the only true and living church upon the face of this earth, of which I bear witness."

PRESIDENT BOYD K. PACKER
Ensign, Dec. 1971, 40–42

1. What doctrines (truths) and principles can you find in this verse?

2. How would you explain to someone why The Church of Jesus Christ of Latter-day Saints is the only true and living church upon the earth?

3. What makes this church "living"?

4. Why is it important to you to know that you belong to the only true and living church upon the earth?

5. What do you think the Lord meant when He stated that He was pleased with His church "collectively and not individually"?

6. What does this scripture teach you about the seminary doctrinal topic: "The Restoration"?

VERSES	OVERVIEW OF WHAT IS HAPPENING OR BEING TAUGHT	WORDS LOOKED UP	INSIGHTS, THOUGHTS, LESSONS LEARNED, DOCTRINES AND PRINCIPLES FOUND
21-23			
24-26			
27-28			
29-30			
31-32			
33-35			
36-38			
39-41			
42-44			
45-47			

TITLE:

VERSES	OVERVIEW OF WHAT IS HAPPENING OR BEING TAUGHT	WORDS LOOKED UP	INSIGHTS, THOUGHTS, LESSONS LEARNED, DOCTRINES AND PRINCIPLES FOUND
48-50			
51-54			
55-58			
59-61			
62-65			
66-67			
68-69			
70-71			
72-73			
74-75			

DOCTRINE & COVENANTS 1 TITLE:

WHEN	WHEN THIS REVELATION WAS GIVEN:	WHERE	WHERE THIS REVELATION WAS GIVEN:	WHY	WHY THIS REVELATION WAS GIVEN:

TIPS

TIP: Whenever the section heading says "HC" with a volume number and page numbers (example in section 1: "HC 1:221-224"), it is referencing the *History of the Church* where you can read the historical account of what was happening (in further detail) at the time the revelation was given.

TIP: Turn back one page in your scriptures to the "Chronological Order of Contents." Find November 1831 and then find section "1." Count the number of revelations (under the "sections" column) that had been received before Doctrine and Covenants 1. Put that number here: _____.
Because most members of the Church did not have access to those revelations you counted above, Joseph held a conference to discuss publishing a book called "The Book of Commandments" with the revelations in them. Doctrine & Covenants 1 is the preface that the Lord revealed for that book.

What is a "preface" and what is its purpose?

1-9

What are some messages the Lord gives at the beginning of this section?

verse 1

verse 2

verse 3

verse 4

verse 5

verse 6

verse 7

verse 8

verse 9

10-16

WARNINGS

What are some messages of warning in these verses?

How might someone prepare themselves for these warnings?

17

CALAMITY:
Great disaster or misfortune; grievous affliction, adversity, misery

What meaning does this verse have to you?

18-39

THE LORD'S PLAN FOR THE CALAMITY

What is the Lord's plan for combatting the calamity of the last days?

DOCTRINE & COVENANTS 1:37-38
THE VOICE OF THE LORD AND HIS SERVANTS IS THE SAME

37 Search these commandments, for they are true and faithful, and the prophecies and promises which are in them shall all be fulfilled.

38 What I the Lord have spoken, I have spoken, and I excuse not myself; and though the heavens and the earth pass away, my word shall not pass away, but shall all be fulfilled, whether by mine own voice or by the voice of my servants, it is the same.

DOCTRINE & COVENANTS 1:37-38

"It is no small thing, my brothers and sisters, to have a prophet of God in our midst. Great and wonderful are the blessings that come into our lives as we listen to the word of the Lord given to us through him. At the same time, knowing that [the President of the Church] is God's prophet also endows us with responsibility. When we hear the counsel of the Lord expressed through the words of the President of the Church, our response should be positive and prompt. History has shown that there is safety, peace, prosperity, and happiness in responding to prophetic counsel as did Nephi of old: 'I will go and do the things which the Lord hath commanded.'

ELDER M. RUSSELL BALLARD
Ensign, May 2001, 40–42

1. What doctrines (truths) and principles can you find in these verses?

2. What instruction is the Lord giving us in these verses?

3. According to verse 37, why should we study the scriptures?

4. Why is it important that you know the "prophecies and promises"?

5. According to verse 38, how lasting and sure are the Lord's words?

6. According to verse 38, what is the same as hearing the Lord's voice?

7. What are some things the prophet today has told you to do?

8. What do these scriptures teach you about the seminary doctrinal topic: "Prophets and Revelation"?

DOCTRINE & COVENANTS 2 TITLE:

WHEN	WHEN THIS SECTION WAS GIVEN:	WHERE	WHERE THIS SECTION WAS GIVEN:	WHY	WHAT WAS HAPPENING WHEN THIS SECTION WAS GIVEN:

What does Joseph Smith learn from Moroni in each of these verses? Record what you find in each box.

2:1	2:2	2:3

What scripture is Moroni quoting?

- -

WHO IS ELIJAH?

What do you learn about Elijah in the Bible Dictionary (look up "Elijah," pay special attention to paragraphs 2 and 4)? Record what you find here:

- -

WHO ARE THE "CHILDREN" AND THE "FATHERS"? WHAT PROMISE DID THE CHILDREN MAKE?

Look up "Family History Work and Genealogy" in *True to the Faith* for help answering this question.

- -

WHY WOULD THE EARTH BE "WASTED" IF THE SEALING POWER WAS NOT RESTORED?

- -

IN THIS SECTION, MORONI APPEARED TO JOSEPH TO MAKE CLEAR A RESPONSIBILITY JOSEPH HAD TO BEAR. WHAT WAS THIS RESPONSIBILITY?

IN CONTEXT OF THIS VERSE, IF MORONI APPEARED TO YOU, WHAT WOULD HE TELL YOU WAS YOUR RESPONSIBILITY?

TITLE:

WHEN THIS REVELATION WAS GIVEN:	WHERE THIS REVELATION WAS GIVEN:	WHAT WAS HAPPENING WHEN THIS REVELATION WAS GIVEN:
WHEN	WHERE	WHY

Study Doctrine and Covenants 3. Each verse has been given a box. Record all of the doctrines and principles you can find in each verse's box.
Include obvious ones and not-so-obvious doctrines and principles.

1	2	3	4
5	6	7	8
9	10	11	12
13	14	15	16 The purpose for the Book of Mormon
17 The purpose for the Book of Mormon	18 The purpose for the Book of Mormon	19 The purpose for the Book of Mormon	20 The purpose for the Book of Mormon

What do you learn from this section about the following doctrines and principles?

ASKING & RECEIVING ANSWERS FROM THE LORD	MAN'S POWERS VS. GOD'S POWERS	THE BOOK OF MORMON

DOCTRINE & COVENANTS 4 TITLE:

WHEN	WHEN THIS REVELATION WAS GIVEN:	WHERE	WHERE THIS REVELATION WAS GIVEN:	WHY	WHAT WAS HAPPENING WHEN THIS REVELATION WAS GIVEN:

VERSES	OVERVIEW OF WHAT IS HAPPENING OR BEING TAUGHT	WORDS LOOKED UP	INSIGHTS, THOUGHTS, LESSONS LEARNED, DOCTRINES AND PRINCIPLES FOUND
1			
2			

WE SHOULD SERVE GOD WITH ALL OF OUR:

WHAT I CAN GIVE

WHAT I THINK IT MEANS TO "SERVE WITH ALL YOUR _____"

HEART

MIGHT

MIND

STRENGTH

3			
4			
5			

WHAT QUALIFIES US FOR THE WORK

WHAT WE MUST HAVE

WHAT THIS IS AND WHY I THINK WE MUST HAVE IT IN ORDER TO BE PART OF THE "MARVELOUS WORK"

FAITH

HOPE

CHARITY

LOVE

EYE SINGLE TO THE GLORY OF GOD

6			
7			

WHAT ARE THESE ATTRIBUTES?

WHY ARE THEY IMPORTANT FOR SERVANTS OF GOD TO POSSESS?

VIRTUE

KNOWLEDGE

TEMPERANCE

PATIENCE

BROTHERLY KINDNESS

GODLINESS

HUMILITY

DILIGENCE

TITLE:

WHEN THIS REVELATION WAS GIVEN:	WHERE THIS REVELATION WAS GIVEN:	WHAT WAS HAPPENING WHEN THIS REVELATION WAS GIVEN:
WHEN	WHERE	WHY At this point, the 116 manuscript pages had been lost. Martin Harris expressed desire to continue to help in the coming forth of the Book of Mormon. Verse 1 reveals what prompted this revelation. Read that verse and write in this box what Martin Harris wanted.

Study Doctrine and Covenants 5. As you study the verses below, record all of the doctrines and principles you can find in each verse's box. Include obvious ones and not-so-obvious doctrines and principles.

1 What Martin Harris wanted	**2** Joseph Smith's responsibility	**3** To whom Joseph can show the plates	**4** Joseph's gift
5-6 Joseph's mission	**7-8** Seeing the plates vs. believing words	**9-10** Why the plates are hidden from the world, & how the world will receive God's word	**11-14** Others who will see the plates
15-16 Those who believe	**17** When the three witnesses will be revealed	**18-20** Warning	**21** MORE uprightly
22 The promise	**23-24** To Martin	**25** Martin's responsibility	**26-27** Martin's instructions & warning
28-29 Martin's choice	**30-31** Instructions to Joseph	**32-33** Why the Lord gives Joseph these instructions	**34-35** Stop, and stand still

WHAT ARE SOME OF THE MOST IMPORTANT LESSONS YOU CAN LEARN FROM THESE SCRIPTURES?

DOCTRINE & COVENANTS 6 TITLE:

WHEN THIS REVELATION WAS GIVEN:	WHERE THIS REVELATION WAS GIVEN:	WHAT WAS HAPPENING WHEN THIS REVELATION WAS GIVEN:
WHEN	WHERE	WHY — Joseph Smith had prayed for someone to help him with the translation of the Book of Mormon. Oliver Cowdery was hired to teach at a school and boarded in the home of Joseph's parents. Joseph Smith Sr. told Oliver about the plates and Oliver prayed about them and felt impressed that he would help Joseph. Oliver met Joseph Smith Jr. on April 5, 1829, and Joseph recognized him as the one who was sent to him. This revelation (Doctrine and Covenants 6) was received soon after Oliver arrived to help Joseph. It contains counsel to Oliver and his role in helping Joseph bring forth the Restoration.

VERSES	DOCTRINES AND PRINCIPLES TAUGHT	WORDS LOOKED UP	INSIGHTS, THOUGHTS, LESSONS LEARNED
1-4			
5-8			
9-11			
12-14			
15-17			
18-21			
22-24			
25-27			
28-31			
32-37			

Look unto me in every thought; doubt not, fear not.

DOCTRINE & COVENANTS 6:36

DOCTRINE & COVENANTS 6:36

LOOK UNTO CHRIST IN EVERY THOUGHT

"We should look to and have our focus firmly fixed upon the Savior at all times and in all places."

ELDER DAVID A. BEDNAR
April 2015 General Conference

1. What do you think it means to look unto Christ in every thought?

2. Circle one of the names below and then write about how that person dealt with difficult situations by staying firmly focused on the Savior.

JOSEPH SMITH JR.
NEPHI
ALMA
MOSES
ESTHER
ABINADI

3. What are some specific ways you can look unto Christ in every thought?

4. How can looking unto Christ in every thought help you when you are experiencing doubt or fear?

5. What does this scripture teach you about the seminary doctrinal topic: "Acquiring Spiritual Knowledge"?

DOCTRINE & COVENANTS 7 TITLE:

WHEN	WHEN THIS REVELATION WAS GIVEN:	WHERE	WHERE THIS REVELATION WAS GIVEN:	WHY	WHAT WAS HAPPENING WHEN THIS REVELATION WAS GIVEN:
					While Joseph and Oliver were working on the translation of the Book of Mormon, they wondered if John the Beloved in the New Testament (the Apostle, not John the Baptist) had died or whether he had been translated and continued to live. This revelation was in response to that question.

VERSES	DOCTRINES AND PRINCIPLES TAUGHT	WORDS LOOKED UP	INSIGHTS, THOUGHTS, LESSONS LEARNED
1			
2			
3			
4			
5			
6			
7			
8			

TITLE:

	WHEN THIS REVELATION WAS GIVEN:	WHERE THIS REVELATION WAS GIVEN:	WHAT WAS HAPPENING WHEN THIS REVELATION WAS GIVEN:
WHEN	**WHERE**	**WHY**	

VERSES	DOCTRINES AND PRINCIPLES TAUGHT	WORDS LOOKED UP	INSIGHTS, THOUGHTS, LESSONS LEARNED
1			
2			
3			
4-5			
6-8			
9-10			
11			
12			

THE GIFT AND SPIRIT OF REVELATION

DOCTRINE & COVENANTS 8:2-3

THE HOLY GHOST SPEAKS TO OUR MINDS AND HEARTS

2 Yea, behold, I will tell you in your mind and in your heart, by the Holy Ghost, which shall come upon you and which shall dwell in your heart.
3 Now, behold, this is the spirit of revelation; behold, this is the spirit by which Moses brought the children of Israel through the Red Sea on dry ground.

DOCTRINE & COVENANTS 8:2-3

"An impression to the mind is very specific.
"Detailed words can be heard or felt and written as though the instruction were being dictated.
"A communication to the heart is a more general impression. The Lord often begins by giving impressions. Where there is a recognition of their importance and they are obeyed, one gains more capacity to receive more detailed instruction to the mind. An impression to the heart, if followed, is fortified by a more specific instruction to the mind" ("Helping Others to Be Spiritually Led" [address to CES religious educators, Aug. 11, 1998], 3–4, LDS.org). **ELDER RICHARD G. SCOTT**

1. Make a list of all of the doctrines and principles you can find in these verses:

2. When Moses arrived at the Red Sea as he led the children of Israel out of Egypt and the Egyptian soldiers came after them, how did Moses think of (and then act upon) separating the waters of the Red Sea and leading the Israelites through the sea?

3. What do you think others might have thought of in that situation? What solutions would come to the average person's mind on how to protect hundreds of thousands of Israelites from the powerful Egyptian army?

4. What can you learn from this? Why is it important for us to understand how to receive revelation?

5. What are some ways the Lord can speak to our minds (as stated in verse 2)?

6. What are some ways the Lord can speak to our hearts (also stated in verse 2)?

7. What do these scriptures teach you about the seminary doctrinal topic: "Acquiring Spiritual Knowledge"?

TITLE:

WHEN	WHERE	WHY
WHEN THIS REVELATION WAS GIVEN:	WHERE THIS REVELATION WAS GIVEN:	WHAT WAS HAPPENING WHEN THIS REVELATION WAS GIVEN:

Oliver had desired the gift to translate and had, for a brief time, been given that gift. That gift was then taken away. Study verses 1-6. Why was that gift removed, and what can you learn from Oliver's experience and the counsel given to him?

verse 1:

verse 2:

verse 3:

verse 4:

verse 5:

verse 6:

PRINCIPLES FOR *Receiving Revelation*

What valuable principles about receiving revelation, and acting upon our gifts, can you find in these verses to Oliver Cowdery?

verse 7:	verse 8:	verse 9:	verse 10:
verse 11:	verse 12:	verse 13:	verse 14:

DOCTRINE & COVENANTS 10 TITLE:

WHEN	WHEN THIS REVELATION WAS GIVEN:	WHERE	WHERE THIS REVELATION WAS GIVEN:	WHY	WHAT WAS HAPPENING WHEN THIS REVELATION WAS GIVEN:

Study Doctrine and Covenants 10. As you study the verses below, record all of the doctrines and principles you can find in each verse's box. Include obvious ones and not-so-obvious doctrines and principles.

1-4 Joseph's gift to translate	5-6 How to overcome Satan and his servants	7 Why Martin was called a wicked man	8-10 What happened to the manuscript
11-13 Satan's plan for the manuscript	14-19 Satan's plan for the manuscript	20-22 How Satan accomplishes his work	23-25 How Satan accomplishes his work
26-27 How Satan accomplishes his work	28-29 How Satan accomplishes his work	30-33 Instructions to Joseph	34-37 Wisdom
38-41 A more particular account	42-43 The Lord's wisdom is greater	44-48 The prophets' and disciples' faith	49-53 A blessing upon this land
54-60 Christ will build up His church	61-65 Christ will build up His church	66-68 More or less than this	69-70 Who will be established upon Christ's rock

Lessons WHAT ARE SOME OF THE MOST IMPORTANT LESSONS YOU CAN LEARN FROM THESE SCRIPTURES?

TITLE:

VERSES	DOCTRINES AND PRINCIPLES TAUGHT	WORDS LOOKED UP	INSIGHTS, THOUGHTS, LESSONS LEARNED
1-3			
4-7			
8-10			
11-14			
15-16			
17-19			
20-21			
22-24			
25-27			
28-30			

DOCTRINE & COVENANTS 12 TITLE:

WHEN THIS REVELATION WAS GIVEN:	WHERE THIS REVELATION WAS GIVEN:	WHAT WAS HAPPENING WHEN THIS REVELATION WAS GIVEN:
WHEN	WHERE	WHY

This revelation is directed to Joseph Knight. He, like other men who have received revelations through Joseph, desired to be righteous and assist in the work. You may notice that the messages in this section have also appeared in previous sections. As you study each verse, answer this question:

WHY IS THIS MESSAGE IMPORTANT FOR A SERVANT OF GOD TO RECEIVE AND UNDERSTAND?

VERSE 1	VERSE 2	VERSE 3

VERSE 4	VERSE 5	VERSE 6

VERSE 7	VERSE 8	VERSE 9

TITLE:

WHEN THIS REVELATION WAS GIVEN:	WHERE THIS REVELATION WAS GIVEN:	WHAT WAS HAPPENING WHEN THIS REVELATION WAS GIVEN:
WHEN	WHERE	WHY — This is the ordination of Joseph Smith and Oliver Cowdery to the Aaronic Priesthood by the hands of John the Baptist.

1- John the Baptist was acting under the direction of whom? Why them? (Use section heading)

2- What else was promised to them in due time? (Use section heading)

3- What does "confer" mean in verse 1?

4- Whose name does John use to give the Priesthood?

5- Who is Aaron and what is the Aaronic Priesthood? (Look up "Aaron" and "Aaronic Priesthood" in the Bible Dictionary)

6- What keys does the Aaronic Priesthood hold?

What do you learn about this event (when the Aaronic Priestood was restored for the first time in this dispensation) from these two sources?

JOSEPH SMITH-HISTORY 1:68-75

JOSEPH SMITH-HISTORY 1:71, FOOTNOTE BY OLIVER COWDERY, LAST TWO PARAGRAPHS

DOCTRINE & COVENANTS 13:1

KEYS OF THE AARONIC PRIESTHOOD

Upon you my fellow servants, in the name of Messiah I confer the Priesthood of Aaron, which holds the keys of the ministering of angels, and of the gospel of repentance, and of baptism by immersion for the remission of sins; and this shall never be taken again from the earth, until the sons of Levi do offer again an offering unto the Lord in righteousness.

DOCTRINE & COVENANTS 13:1

Use the quote to the right to answer the following questions:

1. The verse above is John the Baptist conferring the Aaronic Priesthood for the first time in this dispensation. Who are his "fellow servants"?

2. Why is it important for each young man who holds the Aaronic Priesthood to understand the phrase, "in the name of the Messiah"?

3. What does it mean that a young man who holds the Aaronic Priesthood holds the "keys of the ministering of angels"?

4. What does it mean that a young man who holds the Aaronic Priesthood holds the "keys of the gospel of repentance"?

5. Why is it so significant that a young man who holds the Aaronic Priesthood holds the keys of "baptism by immersion for the remission of sins"?

"When I was a little boy, twelve years of age, and was about to be ordained a deacon, my father challenged me to memorize those words [D&C 13:1]. I did so, and they have remained with me throughout my life....

"Have you ever realized that in the holding and exercise of this priesthood you are a FELLOW SERVANT with John the Baptist, the very man who, while he was alive, baptized Jesus, the Savior of the world and the Son of God, in the waters of the River Jordan?...

"Said he, 'IN THE NAME OF MESSIAH.' None of us exercises this priesthood in the power or authority which we have naturally within ourselves.... I hope you will never forget that in exercising your priesthood as young men, whether in passing the sacrament, in serving as a home teacher, in administering the sacrament, or in baptizing, you are acting as a servant of the Lord in his holy name and by his divine authority.

"Boys, if you will remember this, it will have a tremendous influence upon your lives. You will know that if you are to serve in the name of Jesus Christ, as one holding the priesthood, you cannot with propriety be dishonest, you cannot abuse your bodies with drugs or alcohol or tobacco, you cannot take the name of the Lord in vain, you cannot be morally unclean. You hold the priesthood which authorizes you to act in the name of Jesus Christ. I plead with you tonight to live worthy of the exercise of this priesthood at all times and under all circumstances.

"Then John the Baptist, in his bestowal of this authority, spoke concerning the powers of this priesthood. He said, among other things, that it 'HOLDS THE KEYS OF THE MINISTERING OF ANGELS.'

"When Wilford Woodruff, a man who had lived many years and had many experiences, was the President of the Church, he said to the boys of the Aaronic Priesthood:...'Never in my life, as an Apostle, as a Seventy, or as an Elder, have I ever had more of the protection of the Lord than while holding the office of a Priest.' (Millennial Star, 53:629.)

"Think of it, my dear young brethren. This priesthood which you hold carries with it the keys of the ministering of angels. That means, as I interpret it, that if you live worthy of the priesthood, you have the right to receive and enjoy the very power of heavenly beings to guide you, to protect you, to bless you. What boy, if he is thoughtful, would not welcome this remarkable blessing?...

"The next words given by John to Joseph Smith and Oliver Cowdery — '[THE KEYS] OF THE GOSPEL OF REPENTANCE.'

"Many of you are teachers and priests and have home teaching assignments. You have the authority in this service to be teachers of repentance—that is, to encourage those Latter-day Saints for whom you have some responsibility to live the gospel principles more faithfully. A young man who is a priest comes to my home with his father as a home teacher. He has the opportunity and the responsibility to encourage me to live more fully the principles of the restored gospel of Jesus Christ.

"The great burden of our work in the ministry of the Lord is to teach repentance, to encourage people to resist sin and to walk uprightly before the Lord. This is the gospel of repentance, and yours is the responsibility and the authority under the priesthood which you hold to teach this gospel of repentance. You recognize, of course, that if you are to do so effectively, your own life must be an example.

"And now the next statement of John the Baptist as he conferred the Aaronic Priesthood— '[THE KEYS] OF BAPTISM BY IMMERSION FOR THE REMISSION OF SINS.'

"As all of you who are priests know, you have the authority to baptize by immersion for the remission of sins. Have you ever thought of the wonder of that power?

"If a man or woman has truly repented of his or her sins, then he or she may be eligible to be baptized by immersion with the understanding that those sins will be forgiven and that life can begin anew.

"It is no small or unimportant thing to baptize an individual. You as a young priest, acting in the name of the Lord and under divine authority, wipe out, as it were, by the marvelous process of baptism, the sins of the past and bring about a birth into a new and better life. What a tremendous responsibility you have to live worthy of the exercise of this sacred power!"

PRESIDENT GORDON B. HINCKLEY
October 1982 General Conference

DOCTRINE & COVENANTS 14, 15 & 16

WHEN THIS REVELATION WAS GIVEN:	WHERE THIS REVELATION WAS GIVEN:	WHAT WAS HAPPENING WHEN THIS REVELATION WAS GIVEN:
WHEN	WHERE	WHY — As Joseph Smith and Oliver Cowdery were completing the translation of the Book of Mormon, they came under threat of mob attacks. The Whitmer brothers (David, John, and Peter Jr.) took Joseph and Oliver to their parents' home where they could continue the translation. The brothers desired to know what they could do to help with the work. Each of them received a revelation.

As the Restoration is rolling forth, individuals are being led to Joseph and inspired to be part of this great work. Many of these sections at the beginning of the Doctrine & Covenants are revelations to these individuals, and you will notice many of the messages repeated since they apply to every servant of God. Study each section. Pull out important doctrines and principles that you feel are important for each of these men to understand if they are going to serve God.

DOCTRINE & COVENANTS 14

TO: DAVID WHITMER

Doctrine or principle from section	Why this doctrine or principle is important to know and understand in order to serve God.

DOCTRINE & COVENANTS 15

TO: JOHN WHITMER

DOCTRINE & COVENANTS 16

TO: PETER WHITMER JR.

DOCTRINE & COVENANTS 17 TITLE:

WHEN THIS REVELATION WAS GIVEN:	WHERE THIS REVELATION WAS GIVEN:	WHAT WAS HAPPENING WHEN THIS REVELATION WAS GIVEN:
WHEN	WHERE	WHY

What did Joseph and Oliver learn in these scriptures as they translated the Book of Mormon?

ETHER 5:2-4	2 NEPHI 11:3	2 NEPHI 27:12

Oliver Cowdery, David Whitmer, and Martin Harris desired to be the three special witnesses. What were they told in this revelation Joseph received on this matter?

VERSES	DOCTRINES AND PRINCIPLES TAUGHT	WORDS LOOKED UP	INSIGHTS, THOUGHTS, LESSONS LEARNED
1			
2			
3			
4			
5			
6			
7			
8			
9			

TITLE:

	WHEN THIS REVELATION WAS GIVEN:	WHERE THIS REVELATION WAS GIVEN:		WHAT WAS HAPPENING WHEN THIS REVELATION WAS GIVEN:
WHEN		WHERE	WHY	

VERSES	DOCTRINES AND PRINCIPLES TAUGHT	WORDS LOOKED UP	INSIGHTS, THOUGHTS, LESSONS LEARNED
1-4			
5-8			
9-13			
14-16			
17-22			
23-25			
26-30			
31-36			
37-41			
42-47			

DOCTRINE & COVENANTS 18:10-11

THE WORTH OF SOULS IS GREAT

10 Remember the worth of souls is great in the sight of God;
11 For, behold, the Lord your Redeemer suffered death in the flesh; wherefore he suffered the pain of all men, that all men might repent and come unto him.

DOCTRINE & COVENANTS 18:10-11

"Every person we meet is a VIP [very important person] to our Heavenly Father. Once we understand that, we can begin to understand how we should treat our fellowmen.

"One woman who had been through years of trial and sorrow said through her tears, 'I have come to realize that I am like an old 20-dollar bill—crumpled, torn, dirty, abused, and scarred. But I am still a 20-dollar bill. I am worth something. Even though I may not look like much and even though I have been battered and used, I am still worth the full 20 dollars'"

PRESIDENT DIETER F. UCHTDORF
April 2010 General Conference

1. Make a list of all of the doctrines and principles you can find in these verses:

2. Why do you think you are of such great worth to God?

3. What price did the Savior pay for our souls?

4. Your worth is so great that Jesus Christ suffered and died so you can repent and reach your eternal potential. Why is it important for you and others to understand this?

5. How might this truth influence how you see yourself?

6. How might this truth influence the way you treat other people?

7. If someone believes that the worth of souls is great in the sight of God, then what might his/her belief lead him/her to do?

8. What do these scriptures teach you about the seminary doctrinal topic: "The Atonement of Jesus Christ"?

DOCTRINE & COVENANTS 18:15-16

JOY IN BRINGING SOULS TO JESUS CHRIST

15 And if it so be that you should labor all your days in crying repentance unto this people, and bring, save it be one soul unto me, how great shall be your joy with him in the kingdom of my Father!

16 And now, if your joy will be great with one soul that you have brought unto me into the kingdom of my Father, how great will be your joy if you should bring many souls unto me!

DOCTRINE & COVENANTS 18:15-16

"Crying repentance simply means helping people return to God"

ELDER NEIL L. ANDERSEN
CES fireside address, Jan. 10, 2010

1. Make a list of all of the doctrines and principles you can find in these verses:

2. What do you think it means to "cry repentance"?

3. What are some ways you can help others repent?

4. What blessings are given to those who help others come unto Jesus Christ?

5. Why do you think you will feel joy if you bring others to Jesus Christ?

6. Who are some people in your life who are great examples of these scriptures?

7. What can you do *this week* to be an example of these scriptures?

8. What do these scriptures teach you about the seminary doctrinal topic: "Commandments"?

DOCTRINE & COVENANTS 19 TITLE:

WHEN THIS REVELATION WAS GIVEN:	WHERE THIS REVELATION WAS GIVEN:	WHAT WAS HAPPENING WHEN THIS REVELATION WAS GIVEN:
WHEN	WHERE	Joseph had hired a printing press to print 5000 copies of the Book of Mormon. The cost would be $3000.00 and Martin Harris signed his farm as collateral to guarantee payment to the press. There arose some threats that people would not buy the book so the printer ceased printing the book. Martin became concerned and asked Joseph to approach the Lord on the subject. This revelation followed.

VERSES	DOCTRINES AND PRINCIPLES TAUGHT	WORDS LOOKED UP	INSIGHTS, THOUGHTS, LESSONS LEARNED
1-3			
4-7			
8-9			
10-12			
13-15			
16-17			
18-19			
20			
21-22			
23-24			

VERSES	OVERVIEW OF WHAT IS HAPPENING OR BEING TAUGHT	WORDS LOOKED UP	INSIGHTS, THOUGHTS, LESSONS LEARNED, DOCTRINES AND PRINCIPLES FOUND
25-27			
28-29			
30-33			
34-35			
36-37			
38-39			
40-41			

Lessons

WHAT ARE SOME OF THE MOST IMPORTANT LESSONS YOU CAN LEARN FROM THESE SCRIPTURES?

DOCTRINE & COVENANTS 19:16-19

THE SAVIOR SUFFERED FOR OUR SINS SO WE COULD REPENT

16 For behold, I, God, have suffered these things for all, that they might not suffer if they would repent;
17 But if they would not repent they must suffer even as I;
18 Which suffering caused myself, even God, the greatest of all, to tremble because of pain, and to bleed at every pore, and to suffer both body and spirit—and would that I might not drink the bitter cup, and shrink—
19 Nevertheless, glory be to the Father, and I partook and finished my preparations unto the children of men.

"We will end up either choosing Christ's manner of living or His manner of suffering! It is either 'suffer even as I' , or overcome 'even as [He] … overcame ."

ELDER NEAL A. MAXWELL
April 1987 General Conference

DOCTRINE & COVENANTS 19:16-19

1. Make a list of all of the doctrines and principles you can find in these verses:

2. What will happen to those who choose not to repent for their sins?

3. What reason did the Savior give for why He suffered for our sins?

4. What kind of suffering did the Savior experience?

5. How might knowing about the Savior's suffering have helped Martin Harris as he considered things like the loss of the 116 manuscript pages?

6. When has your knowledge of the Savior's Atonement helped you face something difficult?

7. What do these scriptures teach you about the seminary doctrinal topic: "The Atonement of Jesus Christ"?

TITLE:

WHEN THIS REVELATION WAS GIVEN:	WHERE THIS REVELATION WAS GIVEN:	WHAT WAS HAPPENING WHEN THIS REVELATION WAS GIVEN:
WHEN	WHERE	The Church was officially organized on April 6, 1830. This revelation used to be known as "Articles and Covenants" as it contains a lot of information in order to organize the Church and make clear how the Gospel will be taught and administered to the world. This revelation revealed priesthood offices, ordinances, duties, etc.

Study Doctrine and Covenants 20. As you study the verses below, record all of the doctrines and principles you can find in each verse's box.
Include obvious ones and not-so-obvious doctrines and principles.

1-4 Official organization of Church	5-8 Preparation of Joseph Smith	9-12 The Book of Mormon	13-16 The Book of Mormon
17-20 The Creation & The Fall	21-24 The Atonement & The Resurrection	25-29 Christ desires to save all men	30-36 Warning & Testimony
37 Qualifications for baptism	38-45 Duties of an ELDER	46-52 Duties of a PRIEST	53-56 Duties of a TEACHER
57-59 Duties of a DEACON	60 Power of ordaining	61-67 Conferences	68-69 Duty of members
70 Blessing of children	71-74 The ordinance of baptism	75-79 The ordinance of the sacrament	80-84 Transgressing members and records of members

	WHEN THIS REVELATION WAS GIVEN:		WHERE THIS REVELATION WAS GIVEN:		WHAT WAS HAPPENING WHEN THIS REVELATION WAS GIVEN:
WHEN		WHERE		WHY	This revelation was received at the meeting where the Church was officially organized on April 6, 1830.

VERSES	DOCTRINES AND PRINCIPLES TAUGHT	WORDS LOOKED UP	INSIGHTS, THOUGHTS, LESSONS LEARNED
1-2			
3-4			
5			
6			
7			
8			
9			
10			
11			
12			

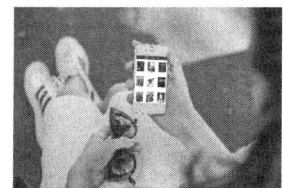

DOCTRINE & COVENANTS 21:4-6

AS WE RECEIVE THE PROPHET'S WORD IN PATIENCE AND FAITH, GOD WILL DISPERSE THE POWERS OF DARKNESS

4 Wherefore, meaning the church, thou shalt give heed unto all his words and commandments which he shall give unto you as he receiveth them, walking in all holiness before me;
5 For his word ye shall receive, as if from mine own mouth, in all patience and faith.
6 For by doing these things the gates of hell shall not prevail against you; yea, and the Lord God will disperse the powers of darkness from before you, and cause the heavens to shake for your good, and his name's glory.

"When we hear the counsel of the Lord expressed through the words of the President of the Church, our response should be positive and prompt. History has shown that there is safety, peace, prosperity, and happiness in responding to prophetic counsel as did Nephi of old: 'I will go and do the things which the Lord hath commanded'"

ELDER M. RUSSELL BALLARD
April 2001 General Conference

DOCTRINE & COVENANTS 21:4-6

1. What doctrines (truths) and principles can you find in these verses?

2. Which of the prophet's teachings are we to heed?

3. Why might it sometimes require patience and faith to heed the words of a prophet?

4. How does knowing that the prophet receives counsel and commandments from the Lord help you to receive his words "in all patience and faith"?

5. How would you summarize the promises given to those who heed the words of the prophet?

6. How does heeding the words of the prophet "disperse the powers of darkness"?

7. Pick a phrase from *For the Strength of Youth* that you believe that, if lived, will bring great blessings into your life, and protect you from the adversary. Write that phrase here:

8. What do these scriptures teach you about the seminary doctrinal topic: "Prophets and Revelation"?

DOCTRINE & COVENANTS 22 TITLE:

	WHEN THIS REVELATION WAS GIVEN:		WHERE THIS REVELATION WAS GIVEN:		WHAT WAS HAPPENING WHEN THIS REVELATION WAS GIVEN:
WHEN		WHERE		WHY	

VERSES	DOCTRINES AND PRINCIPLES TAUGHT	WORDS LOOKED UP	WHAT I LEARNED FROM LOOKING UP THE FOOTNOTES	INSIGHTS, THOUGHTS, LESSONS LEARNED
1				
2				
3				
4				

WHEN THIS REVELATION WAS GIVEN:	WHERE THIS REVELATION WAS GIVEN:	WHAT WAS HAPPENING WHEN THIS REVELATION WAS GIVEN:
WHEN	WHERE	WHY This revelation was given to five men who had an earnest desire to know what God would have them do at this point in their lives and the Church's early stage. Record the five men's names here.

IN THE FIRST COLUMN, RECORD WHAT COUNSEL THE LORD GAVE EACH MAN. IN THE SECOND COLUMN, WRITE YOUR THOUGHTS ABOUT WHAT WE CAN LEARN FROM THAT COUNSEL.

	COUNSEL	WHAT WE CAN LEARN
OLIVER COWDERY VERSES 1-2		
HYRUM SMITH VERSE 3		
SAMUEL SMITH VERSE 4		
JOSEPH SMITH SR. VERSE 5		
JOSEPH KNIGHT SR. VERSES 6-7		

DOCTRINE & COVENANTS 24 TITLE:

WHEN THIS REVELATION WAS GIVEN:	WHERE THIS REVELATION WAS GIVEN:	WHAT WAS HAPPENING WHEN THIS REVELATION WAS GIVEN:
WHEN	**WHERE**	**WHY**

Joseph Smith and Oliver Cowdery were experiencing persecution. Doctrine & Covenants 24, 25 and 26 were given to help comfort and give them instruction on what to do to move foward. Study each verse in section 24. In the first column, record things that you find that would have given Joseph and Oliver comfort and strength during this difficult time. In the second column, record instructions that you find. Not all verses will have both comfort and instruction, and some counsel you may consider to be both comfort and instruction. In the third column, record your thoughts and insights as you are studying.

	Comfort & Strength	Instruction	Thoughts & Insights
1-2			
3-4			
5-6			
7-8			
9-10			
11-12			
13-14			
15-16			
17-18			
19			

TITLE:

WHEN THIS REVELATION WAS GIVEN:	WHERE THIS REVELATION WAS GIVEN:	WHAT WAS HAPPENING WHEN THIS REVELATION WAS GIVEN:
WHEN	**WHERE**	**WHY** Emma Smith (Joseph's wife) had been baptized the month before (June) but was unable to be confirmed until August due to persecution surrounding her family and the Church. This revelation was received to help comfort, strengthen, and give her instruction.

In the first column, record things that you find that would have given Emma comfort and strength during this difficult time. In the second column, record instructions that you find. Not all verses will have both comfort and instruction, and some counsel you may consider to be both comfort and instruction. In the third column, record your thoughts and insights as you are studying.

	Comfort & Strength	Instruction	Thoughts & Insights
1			
2			
3			
4			
5			
6			
7			
8			
9			
10			
11			
12			
13			
14			
15			
16			

DOCTRINE & COVENANTS 26 TITLE:

WHEN THIS REVELATION WAS GIVEN:	WHERE THIS REVELATION WAS GIVEN:	WHAT WAS HAPPENING WHEN THIS REVELATION WAS GIVEN:
WHEN	WHERE	WHY — This was the last of the three revelations given (24, 25, and 26) during time of persecution. All three were intended to comfort, strengthen, and give instruction during that difficult time.

VERSES	DOCTRINES AND PRINCIPLES TAUGHT	WORDS LOOKED UP	INSIGHTS, THOUGHTS, LESSONS LEARNED
1			
2			

Verse 1 instructs them to devote time to studying the scriptures. Look up "scriptures" in *True to the Faith* and/or chapter 2, "How Do I Study Effectively and Prepare to Teach?" in *Preach My Gospel*. Record the things that are meaningful to you and give you greater insight into verse 1.

Scripture Study

TITLE:

WHEN THIS REVELATION WAS GIVEN:	WHERE THIS REVELATION WAS GIVEN:	WHAT WAS HAPPENING WHEN THIS REVELATION WAS GIVEN:
WHEN	WHERE	WHY

Study Doctrine and Covenants 27. As you study the verses below, record all of the doctrines and principles you can find in each verse's box. Include obvious ones and not-so-obvious doctrines and principles.

Instructions for the Sacrament	Instructions for the Sacrament	Prophecy of a future Sacrament Meeting
1-2	3-4	Matthew 26:26-29

Details of this future Sacrament Meeting	Details of this future Sacrament Meeting	Details of this future Sacrament Meeting
5-6	7-11	12-14

Take upon the Lord's whole armor	Take upon the Lord's whole armor	Take upon the Lord's whole armor
15	16-17	18

DOCTRINE & COVENANTS 28 TITLE:

WHEN	WHEN THIS REVELATION WAS GIVEN:	WHERE	WHERE THIS REVELATION WAS GIVEN:	WHY	WHAT WAS HAPPENING WHEN THIS REVELATION WAS GIVEN:

* Pay special attention to what is taught about who is appointed to receive revelation for the entire Church, which was the issue that caused this revelation to be received.

VERSE	DOCTRINES AND PRINCIPLES THIS VERSE IS TEACHING	WORDS LOOKED UP	THOUGHTS, INSIGHTS, AND TESTIMONY
1			
2			
3			
4			
5			
6			
7			
8			
9			
10			
11			
12			
13			
14			
15			
16			

DOCTRINE & COVENANTS 29 TITLE:

WHEN THIS REVELATION WAS GIVEN:	WHERE THIS REVELATION WAS GIVEN:	WHAT WAS HAPPENING WHEN THIS REVELATION WAS GIVEN:
WHEN	WHERE	WHY

THE LORD WILL GATHER HIS PEOPLE

What do you learn about the Lord gathering His people in the following verses?

1-2

3-5

6-7

8-9

10-11

12-13

SIGNS THAT WILL COME BEFORE THE SECOND COMING OF JESUS CHRIST

What do you learn about some of the signs that will precede the Second Coming?

14-15

16-17

18-19

20-21

WHAT WILL HAPPEN AFTER THE MILLENNIUM   What do you learn about some of the signs that will happen after the Millennium?

Look up "Millennium" in *True to the Faith*. Record things you learn about the Millennium (what it is and what will happen) here:

22-23

24-25

26-27

28-29

DOCTRINE   The last part of this section teaches some powerful and profound doctrines. Some may take quite a bit of pondering and study to understand. Study these verses and make a list of doctrines that you find. Highlight the ones that you would like to study further.

30-32

33-35

36-39

40-42

43-46

47-50

DOCTRINE & COVENANTS 29:10-11

CHRIST WILL COME AGAIN WITH POWER AND GLORY

10 For the hour is nigh, and that which was spoken by mine apostles must be fulfilled; for as they spoke so shall it come to pass;

11 For I will reveal myself from heaven with power and great glory, with all the hosts thereof, and dwell in righteousness with men on earth a thousand years, and the wicked shall not stand.

DOCTRINE & COVENANTS 29:10-11

"Your mission will be a sacred opportunity to bring others to Christ and help prepare for the Second Coming of the Savior."

ELDER NEIL L. ANDERSEN
April 2011 General Conference

1. What doctrines (truths) and principles can you find in these verses?

2. Look up and write the definitions for the following words:

NIGH:
FULFILLED:
REVEAL:
HOSTS: a multitude or great number of persons or things

3. What additional insights do those definitions give you?

4. The "thousand years" mentioned in verse 11 are referring to the Millennium. Look up "Millennium" in *True to the Faith* and record five things you learn about the Millennium. If you do not have a *True to the Faith* book, you can find it on the "Gospel Library App" under "Youth," or you can search "True to the Faith" on lds.org.

1–
2–
3–
4–
5–

5. What do these scriptures teach you about the seminary doctrinal topic: "The Godhead"?

30 TITLE:

WHEN THIS REVELATION WAS GIVEN:	WHERE THIS REVELATION WAS GIVEN:	WHAT WAS HAPPENING WHEN THIS REVELATION WAS GIVEN:
WHEN	WHERE	WHY

Doctrine & Covenants 30 was a revelation received for David, Peter, and John Whitmer. In the first column, record doctrines and principles they were taught. In the second column, record your thoughts of how we can learn from this revelation to them.

DOCTRINES & PRINCIPLES TAUGHT	WHAT WE CAN LEARN
DAVID WHITMER VERSES 1-4	
PETER WHITMER JR. VERSES 5-8	
JOHN WHITMER VERSES 9-11	

31 TITLE:

WHEN THIS REVELATION WAS GIVEN:	WHERE THIS REVELATION WAS GIVEN:	WHAT WAS HAPPENING WHEN THIS REVELATION WAS GIVEN:
WHEN	WHERE	WHY

Doctrine & Covenants 31 was a revelation received for Thomas B. Marsh. In the first column, record promises he was given. In the second column, record instructions he was given, and in the third column, record what we can learn from his promises and instructions.

	PROMISES	INSTRUCTIONS	WHAT WE CAN LEARN
1-3			
4-7			
8-11			
12-13			

32 TITLE:

WHEN THIS REVELATION WAS GIVEN:	WHERE THIS REVELATION WAS GIVEN:	WHAT WAS HAPPENING WHEN THIS REVELATION WAS GIVEN:
WHEN	WHERE	WHY

This section contains a mission call to four men to go to western Missouri and preach the Gospel to the Lamanites there. Study each verse. In the left column, record the promises they were given. In the center column, record instructions they were given. And in the third column, record lessons we can learn.

	PROMISES	INSTRUCTIONS	WHAT WE CAN LEARN
1-3			
4-5			

DOCTRINE & COVENANTS 33 TITLE:

WHEN THIS REVELATION WAS GIVEN:	WHERE THIS REVELATION WAS GIVEN:	WHAT WAS HAPPENING WHEN THIS REVELATION WAS GIVEN:
WHEN	WHERE	WHY

Ezra Thayre and Northrop Sweet were both called to preach the Gospel. This revelation instructed them on how to preach the Gospel and what the Lord has done and will yet do. In the first column, record instructions they were given to preach. In the second column, record what the Lord has done. And in the third column, record what we can learn from each verse.

VERSE	HOW TO PREACH THE GOSPEL	WHAT THE LORD HAS DONE AND WILL YET DO	LESSONS WE CAN LEARN
1-3			
4			
5			
6			
7			
8			
9			
10			
11			
12			
13			
14			
15			
16			
17			
18			

TITLE:

	WHEN THIS REVELATION WAS GIVEN:		WHERE THIS REVELATION WAS GIVEN:		WHAT WAS HAPPENING WHEN THIS REVELATION WAS GIVEN:
WHEN		WHERE		WHY	Orson Pratt was a young man of nineteen years old and had demonstrated great faith. This revelation was given to him.

VERSES	DOCTRINES AND PRINCIPLES TAUGHT	WORDS LOOKED UP	INSIGHTS, THOUGHTS, LESSONS LEARNED
1	Note: Notice what the Lord called Orson.		
2-3			
4-5			
6			
7			
8			
9			
10			
11			
12			

DOCTRINE & COVENANTS 35 TITLE:

WHEN	WHEN THIS REVELATION WAS GIVEN:	WHERE	WHERE THIS REVELATION WAS GIVEN:	WHY	WHAT WAS HAPPENING WHEN THIS REVELATION WAS GIVEN:
					Sidney Rigdon, a former minister, met some missionaries in Ohio. Sidney and over 100 people in his congregation were baptized. Sidney went to New York to meet Joseph Smith. After they arrived, Joseph received this revelation.

VERSES	DOCTRINES AND PRINCIPLES TAUGHT	WORDS LOOKED UP	INSIGHTS, THOUGHTS, LESSONS LEARNED
1-2			
3-4			
5-6			
7-8			
9-11			
12-13			
14-16			
17-19			
20-23			
24-27			

36 TITLE:

WHEN THIS REVELATION WAS GIVEN:	WHERE THIS REVELATION WAS GIVEN:	WHAT WAS HAPPENING WHEN THIS REVELATION WAS GIVEN:
WHEN	WHERE	WHY Edward Partridge was a friend of Sidney Rigdon's and had traveled to New York with Sidney to meet Joseph Smith. While he was there, Edward desired to be baptized. Just before he was baptized, Joseph received this revelation.

Study Doctrine and Covenants 36. As you study the verses below, record all of the doctrines and principles you can find in each verse's box. Include obvious ones and not-so-obvious doctrines and principles.

1-2	3-4	5-6	7-8

37 TITLE:

WHEN THIS REVELATION WAS GIVEN:	WHERE THIS REVELATION WAS GIVEN:	WHAT WAS HAPPENING WHEN THIS REVELATION WAS GIVEN:
WHEN	WHERE	WHY

Study Doctrine and Covenants 37. Record the instructions the Lord was giving the Saints in each verse. Include your own thoughts and insights in the boxes.

1	2	3	4

DOCTRINE & COVENANTS 38 TITLE:

WHEN THIS REVELATION WAS GIVEN:	WHERE THIS REVELATION WAS GIVEN:	WHAT WAS HAPPENING WHEN THIS REVELATION WAS GIVEN:
WHEN	WHERE	WHY The Lord had recently commanded his Saints to gather in Ohio. This would mean that the faithful would need to move from their loved ones, farms, homes, and familiar surroundings. This revelation was given at a conference.

As you study these verses, pay special attention to the doctrines and principles taught that would give the Saints courage and peace to help them move from their homes and begin the first gathering of this dispensation.

VERSES	DOCTRINES AND PRINCIPLES TAUGHT	WORDS LOOKED UP	INSIGHTS, THOUGHTS, LESSONS LEARNED
1-3			
4-6			
7-9			
10-12			
13-17			
18-22			
23-27			
28-32			
33-37			
38-42			

WHEN	WHEN THIS REVELATION WAS GIVEN:	WHERE	WHERE THIS REVELATION WAS GIVEN:	WHY	WHAT WAS HAPPENING WHEN THIS REVELATION WAS GIVEN:
					James Covill had been a Baptist minister for over 40 years and had met with Joseph Smith and covenanted to obey any command that the Lord would give him through Joseph. Section 39 is a result of that desire. However, the next day, James returned to his former religion. Section 40 is an explanation of why this happened.

Study Doctrine and Covenants 39-40. As you study the verses below, record all of the doctrines and principles you can find in each verse's box. Include obvious ones and not-so-obvious doctrines and principles.

1-4 Jesus' introduction	5-6 The Gospel	7-9 The Lord knows James	10-14 James' call
15-16 The people in Ohio	17-18 The people in Ohio	19-20 The people in Ohio	21-24 Promises

DOCTRINE & COVENANTS 40	1 James Covill's heart	2 Satan's temptation	3 The broken covenant
* After Joseph received the revelation for James, James forsook his covenant and returned to his former life. This is the Lord's response to Joseph's inquiry as to why this happened. ⟶			

Lessons

WHAT ARE SOME OF THE MOST IMPORTANT LESSONS YOU CAN LEARN FROM THESE SECTIONS?

DOCTRINE & COVENANTS 41 TITLE:

WHEN THIS REVELATION WAS GIVEN:	WHERE THIS REVELATION WAS GIVEN:	WHAT WAS HAPPENING WHEN THIS REVELATION WAS GIVEN:
WHEN	WHERE	WHY Joseph and other Saints now live in Ohio. The Lord had promised them that He would give the Saints His law when they were gathered in Ohio. In this section, He starts instructing them on how to receive His law.

VERSES	DOCTRINES AND PRINCIPLES TAUGHT	WORDS LOOKED UP	INSIGHTS, THOUGHTS, LESSONS LEARNED
1-2			
3-4			
5			
6			
7			
8			
9			
10			
11			
12			

TITLE:

WHEN THIS REVELATION WAS GIVEN:	WHERE THIS REVELATION WAS GIVEN:	WHAT WAS HAPPENING WHEN THIS REVELATION WAS GIVEN:
WHEN	WHERE	WHY — This Section is known as "The Law of the Church." In response to the last revelation they received (41:3), 12 men assembled themselves and prayed to receive the Lord's law. This revelation was a result of that.

Study Doctrine and Covenants 42. As you study the verses below, record all of the doctrines and principles you can find in each verse's box. Include obvious ones and not-so-obvious doctrines and principles.

1-3 Greeting to 12 elders	4-7 The first commandment	8-9 The first commandment	10 Edward Partridge becomes first bishop
11-12 The importance of ordination & what to teach	13-17 Teach by the Spirit	18-29 The commandments	30-34 Consecration
35-39 Consecration	40-42 Character	43-47 Healing of sick and dealing with death	48-55 Power of faith and character
56-60 Know the scriptures and use them to govern the Church	61 Revelation	62-69 New Jerusalem & receiving mysteries	70-73 Use of consecrated property
74-78 Sin	79-82 Sin	83-87 Sin	88-93 Offense

DOCTRINE & COVENANTS 42:11

THE LORD'S REPRESENTATIVES MUST BE CALLED BY ONE WHO HAS AUTHORITY

Again I say unto you, that it shall not be given to any one to go forth to preach my gospel, or to build up my church, except he be ordained by some one who has authority, and it is known to the church that he has authority and has been regularly ordained by the heads of the church.

DOCTRINE & COVENANTS 42:11

"We always know who is called to lead or to teach and have the opportunity to sustain or to oppose the action. It did not come as an invention of man but was set out in the revelations … ([see] D&C 42:11). In this way, the Church is protected from any imposter who would take over a quorum, a ward, a stake, or the Church."

PRESIDENT BOYD K. PACKER
October 2007 General Conference

1. What doctrines (truths) and principles can you find in this verse?

2. Who did the Lord say is authorized to teach and to build up His church?

3. Imagine that you are sitting in the chapel waiting for sacrament meeting to begin. The members of the bishopric or branch presidency have been delayed and have not yet arrived. Someone from the congregation gets up and explains that he would like to extend a few callings and teach some new doctrine that has been revealed to him. How would you react in this situation? Why

4. According to verse 11, those who are called to teach the gospel are to have their callings made known to the Church. How do Church members today learn that a person has received a ward or stake calling and will be set apart or ordained by Church leaders?

5. Why is this a good pattern? How does this protect the Church and the members?

6. What does this scripture teach you about the seminary doctrinal topic: "Priesthood and Priesthood Keys"?

43 TITLE:

	WHEN THIS REVELATION WAS GIVEN:	WHERE THIS REVELATION WAS GIVEN:	WHAT WAS HAPPENING WHEN THIS REVELATION WAS GIVEN:
WHEN			
WHERE			
WHY			When Joseph Smith moved to Kirtland, Ohio, he discovered that some Saints were making false claims about receiving revelation for the Church. Joseph approached the Lord with this problem and section 43 contains the revelation he received.

VERSES	DOCTRINES AND PRINCIPLES TAUGHT	WORDS LOOKED UP	INSIGHTS, THOUGHTS, LESSONS LEARNED
1-7			
8-10			
11-14			
15-16			
17-20			
21-22			
23-24			
25-28			
29-31			
32-35			

44 TITLE:

	WHEN THIS REVELATION WAS GIVEN:	WHERE THIS REVELATION WAS GIVEN:	WHAT WAS HAPPENING WHEN THIS REVELATION WAS GIVEN:
WHEN			
WHERE			
WHY			Section 44 was given as instructions to the Priesthood on how to meet together, preach the Gospel, and feed the poor.

VERSES	DOCTRINES AND PRINCIPLES TAUGHT	WORDS LOOKED UP	INSIGHTS, THOUGHTS, LESSONS LEARNED
1			
2			
3			
4			
5			
6			

DOCTRINE & COVENANTS 45 TITLE:

WHEN	WHEN THIS REVELATION WAS GIVEN:	WHERE	WHERE THIS REVELATION WAS GIVEN:	WHY	WHAT WAS HAPPENING WHEN THIS REVELATION WAS GIVEN:

Study Doctrine and Covenants 45. As you study the verses below, record all of the doctrines and principles you can find in each verse's box. Include obvious ones and not-so-obvious doctrines and principles.

1-5 Christ's roles	**6-10** Listen and receive everlasting covenant	**11-15** Be like Enoch	**16-20** Signs of the Second Coming
21-23 Signs of the Second Coming	**24-25** Scattering & gathering of Israel	**26-28** The Gospel is restored	**29-31** Many will not receive the Gospel
32-33 Stand in holy places	**34-38** Be not troubled. Watch and be prepared.	**39-42** Signs of the Second Coming	**43-45** The Second Coming
46 The Resurrection at the time of the Second Coming	**47-50** Christ at the Mount of Olives	**51-53** The Jews will recognize Christ as the Messiah	**54-55** First Resurrection and Satan bound
56-59 Parable of Ten Virgins fulfilled	**60-62** Joseph Smith to begin translation of the New Testament (JST)	**63-66** Gather and build the New Jerusalem	**67-75** Safety of Zion

WHEN THIS REVELATION WAS GIVEN:	WHERE THIS REVELATION WAS GIVEN:	WHAT WAS HAPPENING WHEN THIS REVELATION WAS GIVEN:
WHEN	WHERE	WHY At this time, the Saints had only been allowing members and interested investigators into their Church meetings. The Lord tells them to allow others into their meetings. The Lord also teaches them about the gifts of the Spirit.

SPIRITUAL GIFTS Look up "spiritual gifts" in *True to the Faith*. In this space, record a good description of what spiritual gifts are.

VERSES	OVERVIEW OF WHAT IS HAPPENING OR BEING TAUGHT	WORDS LOOKED UP	INSIGHTS, THOUGHTS, LESSONS LEARNED, DOCTRINES AND PRINCIPLES FOUND
1-3			
4-6			
7			
8-9			
10-12			

	GIFTS OF THE SPIRIT	WHAT THIS GIFT IS AND HOW IT CAN BE USED TO BLESS OTHERS
13		
14		
15		
16		
17		
18		
19		
20		
21		
22		
23		
24		
25		

26-28			
29-30			
31-33			

DOCTRINE & COVENANTS 47-48

47 TITLE:

WHEN THIS REVELATION WAS GIVEN:	WHERE THIS REVELATION WAS GIVEN:	WHAT WAS HAPPENING WHEN THIS REVELATION WAS GIVEN:
WHEN	WHERE	WHY — Oliver Cowdery had previously served as the Church historian but was now serving a mission. This revelation is a call to John Whitmer to serve in this capacity.

What are some principles that you can find in this section that can apply to any Church calling any of us receive?

48 TITLE:

WHEN THIS REVELATION WAS GIVEN:	WHERE THIS REVELATION WAS GIVEN:	WHAT WAS HAPPENING WHEN THIS REVELATION WAS GIVEN:
WHEN	WHERE	WHY — Many Saints were gathering to Kirtland as they had been commanded. This revelation addressed the issue of them no longer having land, as they had left their land and homes behind.

VERSES	OVERVIEW OF WHAT IS HAPPENING OR BEING TAUGHT	WORDS LOOKED UP	INSIGHTS, THOUGHTS, LESSONS LEARNED, DOCTRINES AND PRINCIPLES FOUND
1-2			
3			
4			
5			
6			

TITLE:

WHEN	WHEN THIS REVELATION WAS GIVEN:	WHERE	WHERE THIS REVELATION WAS GIVEN:	WHY	WHAT WAS HAPPENING WHEN THIS REVELATION WAS GIVEN:
					Leman Copely was an early convert and had previously been a "Shaker." Shakers are a religion that broke off from the Quakers. Leman desired to preach the Gospel to his former friends who were still practicing his former religion. This revelation was then received.

SHAKERS Using the section heading, what five doctrines do you learn the "Shakers" believed?

❶
❷
❸
❹
❺

VERSES	DOCTRINES AND PRINCIPLES TAUGHT	WORDS LOOKED UP	INSIGHTS, THOUGHTS, LESSONS LEARNED
1-4			
5-7			
8-10			
11-12			
13-14			
15-17			
18-21			
22			
23-25			
26-28			

* After you have completed the study of this section, go through each of the five beliefs the Shakers held and highlight the answers the Lord gave to them.

DOCTRINE & COVENANTS 49:15-17

MARRIAGE BETWEEN A MAN AND A WOMAN IS ORDAINED OF GOD

15 And again, verily I say unto you, that whoso forbiddeth to marry is not ordained of God, for marriage is ordained of God unto man.
16 Wherefore, it is lawful that he should have one wife, and they twain shall be one flesh, and all this that the earth might answer the end of its creation;
17 And that it might be filled with the measure of man, according to his creation before the world was made.

"The most important single thing that any Latter-day Saint ever does in this world is to marry the right person, in the right place, by the right authority."

ELDER BRUCE R. MCCONKIE
"Agency or Inspiration?" New Era, Jan. 1975, 38.

DOCTRINE & COVENANTS 49:15-17

1. What doctrines (truths) and principles can you find in these verses?

2. What do you think it means that God ORDAINS marriage?

3. The phrase *"that the earth might answer the end of its creation; and that it might be filled with the measure of man,"* teaches that one purpose of the earth's creation was to provide a place where God's children could live as families. What are some ways Satan tries to stop this from happening?

4. What purposes does marriage between a man and a woman fulfill in Heavenly Father's plan?

5. How is "forbidd[ing] to marry" counter to Heavenly Father's plan?

6. According to verse 16, God approves of traditional marriage between a man and a woman. What are some ways people attempt to ridicule or destroy traditional marriage?

7. What can young men and young women do now to prepare for celestial marriage?

8. What do these scriptures teach you about the seminary doctrinal topic: "Marriage and Family"?

TITLE:

	WHEN THIS REVELATION WAS GIVEN:	WHERE THIS REVELATION WAS GIVEN:	WHAT WAS HAPPENING WHEN THIS REVELATION WAS GIVEN:
WHEN			
		WHERE	
			WHY

As you study these verses, pay special attention to the doctrines and principles taught that would give the Saints a good understanding between false spirits and the Spirit of Truth.

VERSES	DOCTRINES AND PRINCIPLES TAUGHT	WORDS LOOKED UP	INSIGHTS, THOUGHTS, LESSONS LEARNED
1-3			
4-6			
7-9			
10-12			
13-15			
16-20			
21-23			
24-25			
26-29			
30-33			
34-36			
37-40			
41-46			

DOCTRINE & COVENANTS 51 TITLE:

WHEN	WHEN THIS REVELATION WAS GIVEN:	WHERE	WHERE THIS REVELATION WAS GIVEN:	WHY	WHAT WAS HAPPENING WHEN THIS REVELATION WAS GIVEN:

Edward Partridge was the first bishop. The bishop holds responsibilities over temporal (or physical) well-being of the members he serves. One important responsibility is to administer the welfare program in his ward. As the bishop, Edward Partridge needed to help those Saints that were moving to the Kirtland area. One group was directed to live the law of consecration and this section helped Edward know how to direct such efforts.

VERSES	OVERVIEW OF WHAT IS HAPPENING OR BEING TAUGHT	WORDS LOOKED UP	INSIGHTS, THOUGHTS, LESSONS LEARNED, DOCTRINES AND PRINCIPLES FOUND
1			
2			

LAW OF CONSECRATION

VERSES	PRINCIPLES OF THE LAW OF CONSECRATION
3	
4	
5-6	
7	
8	
9	
10-12	
13	
14	
15	
16	

VERSES	OVERVIEW OF WHAT IS HAPPENING OR BEING TAUGHT	WORDS LOOKED UP	INSIGHTS, THOUGHTS, LESSONS LEARNED, DOCTRINES AND PRINCIPLES FOUND
17-20			

WHEN THIS REVELATION WAS GIVEN:	WHERE THIS REVELATION WAS GIVEN:	WHAT WAS HAPPENING WHEN THIS REVELATION WAS GIVEN:
WHEN	**WHERE**	**WHY** Joseph Smith had just closed the fourth conference of the Church. In this revelation, the Lord tells them that the next conference should be held in Missouri and that as they travel they should preach along the way. The Lord then designates the companionships and gives them instruction on how not to be deceived by Satan.

VERSES	DOCTRINES AND PRINCIPLES TAUGHT	WORDS LOOKED UP	INSIGHTS, THOUGHTS, LESSONS LEARNED
1-2			
3-6			
7-11			
12-14			
	The Pattern: That Ye May Not Be Deceived 15: 16: 17:		
18-20			

Record the names of each set of missionary companions. The number is the verse the companions are found in. Each box should have two names.

MISSIONARY COMPANIONS

⑦	㉔ Joseph Smith Jr. & Sidney Rigdon	㉙
⑧	㉕	㉚
㉒	㉖	㉛
㉓	㉗	㉜
㉔	㉘	㉟

VERSES	INSTRUCTIONS GIVEN TO MISSIONARIES:	WORDS LOOKED UP	INSIGHTS, THOUGHTS, LESSONS LEARNED
33			
34			
36-38			

* While the missionary companionships were leaving to preach, other men stayed behind in Ohio. Notice the responsibilities put on these men.

VERSES	INSTRUCTIONS AND RESPONSIBILITIES OF MEN STAYING IN OHIO	WORDS LOOKED UP	INSIGHTS, THOUGHTS, LESSONS LEARNED
39-40			

	PROMISES FOR MISSOURI		
41-44			

DOCTRINE & COVENANTS 53-55

53 TITLE:

	WHEN THIS REVELATION WAS GIVEN:		WHERE THIS REVELATION WAS GIVEN:		WHAT WAS HAPPENING WHEN THIS REVELATION WAS GIVEN:
WHEN		WHERE		WHY	

VERSES	INSTRUCTIONS, DOCTRINES, & PRINCIPLES	WORDS LOOKED UP	INSIGHTS, THOUGHTS, LESSONS LEARNED
53:1-2			
53:3-4			
53:5-7			

54 TITLE:

	WHEN THIS REVELATION WAS GIVEN:		WHERE THIS REVELATION WAS GIVEN:		WHAT WAS HAPPENING WHEN THIS REVELATION WAS GIVEN:
WHEN		WHERE		WHY	

VERSES	INSTRUCTIONS, DOCTRINES, & PRINCIPLES	WORDS LOOKED UP	INSIGHTS, THOUGHTS, LESSONS LEARNED
54:1-3			
54:4-7			
54:8-10			

55 TITLE:

	WHEN THIS REVELATION WAS GIVEN:		WHERE THIS REVELATION WAS GIVEN:		WHAT WAS HAPPENING WHEN THIS REVELATION WAS GIVEN:
WHEN		WHERE		WHY	

VERSES	INSTRUCTIONS, DOCTRINES, & PRINCIPLES	WORDS LOOKED UP	INSIGHTS, THOUGHTS, LESSONS LEARNED
55:1-2			
55:3-4			
55:5-6			

TITLE:

	WHEN THIS REVELATION WAS GIVEN:	WHERE THIS REVELATION WAS GIVEN:	WHAT WAS HAPPENING WHEN THIS REVELATION WAS GIVEN:
WHEN		**WHERE**	**WHY** Ezra Thayre was one of the men called on a mission in section 52. He was to be companions with Thomas B. Marsh. Due to a dispute over some property in Thompson, Ohio, Elder Thayre was not ready to leave when Elder Marsh was prepared to go.

VERSE	DOCTRINES AND PRINCIPLES TAUGHT	WORDS LOOKED UP	LESSONS WE CAN LEARN
1-3			
4-5			
6-7			
8			
9			
10			
11			
12			
13			
14			
15			
16			
17			
18			
19			
20			

DOCTRINE & COVENANTS 57 TITLE:

WHEN	WHEN THIS REVELATION WAS GIVEN:	WHERE	WHERE THIS REVELATION WAS GIVEN:	WHY	WHAT WAS HAPPENING WHEN THIS REVELATION WAS GIVEN:
					By this point, many Saints had begun to move to Missouri. They still had little information on Zion and where, specifically, it would be. This revelation revealed the center point of Zion as well as what the Saints could do to move the work forward.

Study Doctrine and Covenants 57. Record the information and instruction the Lord gives the Saints concerning Zion and moving the work forward.

1	2	3	4
5	6	7	8
9	10	11	12
13	14	15	16

TITLE:

	WHEN THIS REVELATION WAS GIVEN:	WHERE THIS REVELATION WAS GIVEN:	WHAT WAS HAPPENING WHEN THIS REVELATION WAS GIVEN:
WHEN			
WHERE			
WHY			Saints were continuing to gather to Missouri while the Lord had others stay in Ohio. As the Saints were arriving, they were anxious to know the will of the Lord for them and the land in Missouri.

VERSES	DOCTRINES AND PRINCIPLES TAUGHT	WORDS LOOKED UP	INSIGHTS, THOUGHTS, LESSONS LEARNED
1-3			
4-5			
6-7			
8-12			
13-16			
17-20			
21-25			
26-28			
29-30			
31-33			

VERSES	DOCTRINES AND PRINCIPLES TAUGHT	WORDS LOOKED UP	INSIGHTS, THOUGHTS, LESSONS LEARNED
34-36			
37-39			
40-43			
44-46			
47-49			
50-52			
53-55			
56-58			
59-61			
62-65			

DOCTRINE & COVENANTS 58:42 - 43

TO REPENT WE MUST CONFESS AND FORSAKE SIN

42 Behold, he who has repented of his sins, the same is forgiven, and I, the Lord, remember them no more.
43 By this ye may know if a man repenteth of his sins—behold, he will confess them and forsake them.

DOCTRINE & COVENANTS 58:42-43

"Satan will try to make us believe that our sins are not forgiven because we can remember them. Satan is a liar; he tries to blur our vision and lead us away from the path of repentance and forgiveness. God did not promise that we would not remember our sins. Remembering will help us avoid making the same mistakes again. But if we stay true and faithful, the memory of our sins will be softened over time. This will be part of the needed healing and sanctification process"

PRESIDENT DIETER F. UCHTDORF
April 2007 General Conference

1. What doctrines (truths) and principles can you find in these verses?

2. According to these verses, what does the Lord promise us if we repent of our sins?

3. Which of our sins does this promise apply to?

4. According to verse 43, How can you know if someone repents?

5. What do you think it means when someone confesses and forsakes their sins?

6. Look up "Repentance" in *True to the Faith* and record five things you learn about the Millennium. If you do not have a *True to the Faith* book, you can find it on the "Gospel Library App" under "Youth," or you can search "True to the Faith" on lds.org.

1–
2–
3–
4–
5–

7. What do these scriptures teach you about the seminary doctrinal topic: "The Atonement of Jesus Christ"?

DOCTRINE & COVENANTS 59 TITLE

WHEN	WHEN THIS REVELATION WAS GIVEN:	WHERE	WHERE THIS REVELATION WAS GIVEN:	WHY	WHAT WAS HAPPENING WHEN THIS REVELATION WAS GIVEN:

VERSES	DOCTRINES AND PRINCIPLES TAUGHT	WORDS LOOKED UP	INSIGHTS, THOUGHTS, LESSONS LEARNED
1-2			
3-4			
5			
6-8			
9-10			
11			
12-13			
14-15			
16-19			
20			
21			
22			
23-24			

60 TITLE:

WHEN THIS REVELATION WAS GIVEN:	WHERE THIS REVELATION WAS GIVEN:	WHAT WAS HAPPENING WHEN THIS REVELATION WAS GIVEN:
WHEN	WHERE	WHY After being in Missouri, it was time for many of the elders to return to Ohio. This revelation gives them instruction for their travels.

VERSES	OVERVIEW OF WHAT IS HAPPENING OR BEING TAUGHT	WORDS LOOKED UP	INSIGHTS, THOUGHTS, LESSONS LEARNED, DOCTRINES AND PRINCIPLES FOUND
1-3			
4-6			
7-11			
12-14			
15-17			

61 TITLE:

WHEN THIS REVELATION WAS GIVEN:	WHERE THIS REVELATION WAS GIVEN:	WHAT WAS HAPPENING WHEN THIS REVELATION WAS GIVEN:
WHEN	WHERE	WHY On the third day of their travels (traveling by canoe), the elders experienced danger while upon the Missouri River. The next morning, Joseph received this revelation.

1-5			
6-12			
13-17			
18-22			
23-29			
30-35			
36-39			

62 TITLE:

WHEN THIS REVELATION WAS GIVEN:	WHERE THIS REVELATION WAS GIVEN:	WHAT WAS HAPPENING WHEN THIS REVELATION WAS GIVEN:
WHEN	WHERE	WHY The day after the incident upon the river, the elders met several other elders who were coming from Ohio on their way to Missouri. It was a joyful meeting. Joseph received this revelation on their behalf.

1-2			
3			
4-5			
6-7			
8-9			

DOCTRINE & COVENANTS 63 TITLE:

	WHEN THIS REVELATION WAS GIVEN:		WHERE THIS REVELATION WAS GIVEN:		WHAT WAS HAPPENING WHEN THIS REVELATION WAS GIVEN:
WHEN		WHERE		WHY	

Study this section. As you study the verses below, record all of the doctrines and principles you can find in each verse's box. Include obvious ones and not-so-obvious doctrines and principles.

1-4 Open your hearts and prepare to hear	5-6 The day of wrath shall come	7-8 Sign seekers	9-10 Faith
11-12 Faith unto mighty works	13-16 Repent speedily	17-19 Second Death	20-23 Earth transfigured & mysteries
24-26 The Lord holds Zion, but still respects law of land	27-31 Purchase lands	32-35 Evil upon Earth, the Lord is with the Saints	36-37 Assemble yourselves and warn others
38-41 Temporal concerns	42-46 Newel K. Whitney	47-48 Blessings for the faithful	49-52 The dead and the living at the Second Coming
53-54 Look for these things	55-57 Desire to hold Priesthood	58-63 Day of warning	64-66 What cometh from above is sacred

TITLE:

WHEN THIS REVELATION WAS GIVEN:	WHERE THIS REVELATION WAS GIVEN:	WHAT WAS HAPPENING WHEN THIS REVELATION WAS GIVEN:
WHEN	WHERE	On the previous journey to and from Missouri, some of the elders had experienced disagreements with one another but had worked through them. Now, as some more brethren were getting ready to depart on the same journey, Joseph received this revelation.

VERSES	DOCTRINES AND PRINCIPLES TAUGHT	WORDS LOOKED UP	INSIGHTS, THOUGHTS, LESSONS LEARNED
1-4			
5-7			
8-11			
12-14			
15-18			
19-21			
22-25			
26-30			
31-32			
33-34			
35-38			
39-40			
41-43			

9 Wherefore, I say unto you, that ye ought to forgive one another; for he that forgiveth not his brother his trespasses standeth condemned before the Lord; for there remaineth in him the greater sin. 10 I, the Lord, will forgive whom I will forgive, but of you it is required to forgive all men. 11 And ye ought to say in your hearts—let God judge between me and thee, and reward thee according to thy deeds.

DOCTRINE & COVENANTS 64:9-11

DOCTRINE & COVENANTS 64:9-11

WE ARE REQUIRED TO FORGIVE ALL PEOPLE

"I plead with you to ask the Lord for strength to forgive. … It may not be easy, and it may not come quickly. But if you will seek it with sincerity and cultivate it, it will come."

PRESIDENT GORDON B. HINCKLEY
Ensign, June 1991, 5

1. What doctrines (truths) and principles can you find in these verses?

2. According to verse 9, what is a consequence of refusing to forgive others?

3. What commandment does the Lord give in verse 10?

4. Why do you think it is important to forgive all people, regardless of whether they apologize for their wrongdoings?

5. How can verse 11 help us forgive others?

6. What did President Hinckley counsel us to do if we are struggling to forgive someone (see quote at top of page)? How do you think praying for strength can help us to forgive?

7. What do these scriptures teach you about the seminary doctrinal topic: "Commandments"?

65 TITLE:

WHEN THIS REVELATION WAS GIVEN:	WHERE THIS REVELATION WAS GIVEN:	WHAT WAS HAPPENING WHEN THIS REVELATION WAS GIVEN:
WHEN	**WHERE**	**WHY** Joseph and his family moved from Kirtland to Hiram, Ohio. They moved in with the Johnson family. Once he was there, he received this revelation.

As you study this section, look at each verse and pull out truths (doctrine) that are taught and record them in the left column. Also, look for specific instructions given from the Lord and record those in the right column. Some verses may not have both doctrine and instructions, so you may have lines empty.

DOCTRINE TAUGHT IN THESE VERSES	INSTRUCTIONS GIVEN
VERSE 1	
VERSE 2	
VERSE 3	
VERSE 4	
VERSE 5	
VERSE 6	

66 TITLE:

WHEN THIS REVELATION WAS GIVEN:	WHERE THIS REVELATION WAS GIVEN:	WHAT WAS HAPPENING WHEN THIS REVELATION WAS GIVEN:
WHEN	**WHERE**	**WHY** This revelation was for William E. McLellin, who had been recently baptized. He asked Joseph to inquire of the Lord on his behalf. This is the revelation that followed.

William E. McLellin will later leave the Church. The Lord, knowing his weakness, gives him personal and specifc instructions and counsel in this section. Go through each verse and record the teachings in the left column. In the right column, record your thoughts about how important those teachings are. Pay particular attention to the teachings you feel that, if embraced, would have helped keep William in the path of righteousness.

TEACHINGS AND INSTRUCTION	PERSONAL THOUGHTS AND INSIGHTS
VERSE 1	
VERSE 2	
VERSE 3	
VERSE 4	
VERSE 5	
VERSE 6	
VERSE 7	
VERSE 8	
VERSE 9	
VERSE 10	
VERSE 11	
VERSE 12	
VERSE 13	

DOCTRINE & COVENANTS 67 TITLE:

WHEN THIS REVELATION WAS GIVEN:	WHERE THIS REVELATION WAS GIVEN:	WHAT WAS HAPPENING WHEN THIS REVELATION WAS GIVEN:
WHEN	**WHERE**	**WHY** This revelation came just after Doctrine & Covenants 1, or the Preface to *The Book of Commandments*. They had just held a conference where they had decided to publish the revelations received up to this point. After decisions had been made on how to proceed with the publication, the Prophet heard that some of the brethren were questioning the language used in the revelations.

VERSES	DOCTRINES AND PRINCIPLES TAUGHT	WORDS LOOKED UP	INSIGHTS, THOUGHTS, LESSONS LEARNED
67:1-2			
67:3-5			
67:6-7			
67:8-10			
67:11-13			
67:14			

DOCTRINE & COVENANTS 68

TITLE:

WHEN	WHERE	WHY
WHEN THIS REVELATION WAS GIVEN:	WHERE THIS REVELATION WAS GIVEN:	WHAT WAS HAPPENING WHEN THIS REVELATION WAS GIVEN: Four men who were at the conference discussing the publication of the Book of Commandments requested that Joseph inquire of the Lord on their behalf. This revelation followed.

VERSES	DOCTRINES AND PRINCIPLES TAUGHT	WORDS LOOKED UP	INSIGHTS, THOUGHTS, LESSONS LEARNED
1-2			
3-5			
6-7			
8-10			
11-12			
13-15			
16-18			
19-20			
21-23			
24-26			
27-29			
30-31			
32-35			

DOCTRINE & COVENANTS 69-71

69 TITLE:

WHEN THIS REVELATION WAS GIVEN:	WHERE THIS REVELATION WAS GIVEN:	WHAT WAS HAPPENING WHEN THIS REVELATION WAS GIVEN:
WHEN	WHERE	WHY Oliver Cowdery had been given the assignment to carry the manuscript for *The Book of Commandments* to W.W. Phelps who would print the book in Independence, Missouri. He needed a traveling companion so this revelation was given.

Study these verses and record the instructions that Oliver Cowdery and John Whitmer received in the "instructions" column, and the promises given to them in the "promises" column.

VERSES	INSTRUCTIONS	PROMISES
69:1-3		
69:4-6		
69:7-8		

70 TITLE:

WHEN THIS REVELATION WAS GIVEN:	WHERE THIS REVELATION WAS GIVEN:	WHAT WAS HAPPENING WHEN THIS REVELATION WAS GIVEN:
WHEN	WHERE	WHY In this revelation, the Lord chooses 6 stewards to publish *The Book of Commandments*.

WHO THE STEWARDS ARE AND WHAT THEY HAVE BEEN APPOINTED TO DO	COUNSEL TO THOSE WITH A STEWARDSHIP	TEMPORAL EXPECTATIONS OF SAINTS
70:1-5	70:6-13	70:14-18

71 TITLE:

WHEN THIS REVELATION WAS GIVEN:	WHERE THIS REVELATION WAS GIVEN:	WHAT WAS HAPPENING WHEN THIS REVELATION WAS GIVEN:
WHEN	WHERE	WHY

VERSES	INSTRUCTIONS, DOCTRINES & PRINCIPLES	WORDS LOOKED UP	INSIGHTS, THOUGHTS, LESSONS LEARNED
71:1-3			
71:4-7			
71:8-11			

WHEN	WHEN THIS REVELATION WAS GIVEN:	WHERE	WHERE THIS REVELATION WAS GIVEN:	WHY	WHAT WAS HAPPENING WHEN THIS REVELATION WAS GIVEN:

As you study this section, record what you learn about the following things in the proper boxes.

Rendering accounts of stewardship	The Bishop's Storehouse	Bishops to certify worthiness of elders
72:1-8	72:9-15	72:16-26

WHEN	WHEN THIS REVELATION WAS GIVEN:	WHERE	WHERE THIS REVELATION WAS GIVEN:	WHY	WHAT WAS HAPPENING WHEN THIS REVELATION WAS GIVEN:

As you study this section, record what you learn about the following things in the proper boxes.

Instructions for elders	Instructions for Joseph and Sidney
73:1-2	73:3-6

WHEN	WHEN THIS REVELATION WAS GIVEN:	WHERE	WHERE THIS REVELATION WAS GIVEN:	WHY	WHAT WAS HAPPENING WHEN THIS REVELATION WAS GIVEN:
					In this revelation, the Lord explains 1 Corinthians 7:14 which had been used by some religions to show the need of baptizing infants.

Summarize the explanation the Lord gave for this scripture.

1 Corinthians 7:14

For the unbelieving husband is sanctified by the wife, and the unbelieving wife is sanctified by the husband: else were your children unclean; but now are they holy.

1-3

4-5

6-7

DOCTRINE & COVENANTS 75 TITLE:

	WHEN THIS REVELATION WAS GIVEN:		WHERE THIS REVELATION WAS GIVEN:		WHAT WAS HAPPENING WHEN THIS REVELATION WAS GIVEN:
WHEN		WHERE		WHY	

VERSES	DOCTRINES AND PRINCIPLES TAUGHT	WORDS LOOKED UP	INSIGHTS, THOUGHTS, LESSONS LEARNED
1-3			
4-5			
6-9			
10-12			
13-14			
15-18			
19-20			
21-22			
23-24			
25-26			
27-28			
29			
30-36			

TITLE:

WHEN THIS REVELATION WAS GIVEN:	WHERE THIS REVELATION WAS GIVEN:	WHAT WAS HAPPENING WHEN THIS REVELATION WAS GIVEN:
WHEN	WHERE	WHY

Study this section. As you study the verses below, record all of the doctrines and principles you can find in each verse's box. Include obvious ones and not-so-obvious doctrines and principles.

1-4 The Lord is God	5-6 Promise to the righteous	7-8 Mysteries will be revealed	9-10 Gaining great wisdom
11-14 The record of the vision	**15-17 John 5:29**	**18-19 Power of meditation**	**20-24 Vision of Heavenly Father & Jesus Christ**
25-27 Fall of Lucifer	**28-29 Satan makes war**	**30-32 Sons of Perdition**	**33-36 Sons of Perdition**
37-38 Sons of Perdition	**39-42 All others will be saved**	**43-44 Sons of Perdition will not be saved**	**45-48 Outer Darkness**
49 Write the vision	**50-52 Celestial Beings**	**53-56 Celestial Beings**	**57-59 Celestial Beings**

| 60-63 | Celestial Beings | 64-65 | Celestial Beings | 66-68 | Celestial Beings | 69-70 | Celestial Beings |

| 71 | Terrestrial Beings | 72-74 | Terrestrial Beings | 75-77 | Terrestrial Beings | 78-79 | Terrestrial Beings |

| 80 | Write the vision | 81 | Telestial Beings | 82-83 | Telestial Beings | 84-85 | Telestial Beings |

| 86-88 | Telestial Beings | 89-90 | Telestial Beings | 91 | Terrestrial Beings | 92 | Celestial Beings |

| 93-95 | Celestial World | 96 | Celestial Beings | 97 | Terrestrial Beings | 98 | Telestial Beings |

99-101 Telestial Beings	102-104 Telestial Beings	105-107 Telestial Beings	108-110 Telestial Beings

111-112 Telestial Beings	113 Write the vision	114-116 Only understood by Spirit	117-119 Only understood by Spirit

Lessons

WHAT ARE SOME OF THE MOST IMPORTANT LESSONS YOU CAN LEARN FROM THIS SECTION?

JESUS CHRIST LIVES AND IS THE CREATOR OF WORLDS

22 And now, after the many testimonies which have been given of him, this is the testimony, last of all, which we give of him: That he lives!

23 For we saw him, even on the right hand of God; and we heard the voice bearing record that he is the Only Begotten of the Father—

24 That by him, and through him, and of him, the worlds are and were created, and the inhabitants thereof are begotten sons and daughters unto God.

DOCTRINE & COVENANTS 76:22-24

"This testimony is now, as it has always been, a declaration, a straightforward assertion of truth as we know it. Simple and powerful is the statement of Joseph Smith and Sidney Rigdon concerning the Lord, who stands at the head of this work."

PRESIDENT GORDON B. HINCKLEY
April 1998 General Conference

1. What doctrines (truths) do these verses teach about Jesus Christ?

2. Which of these truths are you especially grateful for and why?

3. Which of these doctrines can you testify of? How do you know it is true?

4. Complete this sentence: Regarding Jesus Christ, I know …

5. How have these truths impacted your life?

6. What do these scriptures teach you about the seminary doctrinal topic: "The Plan of Salvation"?

TITLE:

WHEN THIS REVELATION WAS GIVEN:	WHERE THIS REVELATION WAS GIVEN:	WHAT WAS HAPPENING WHEN THIS REVELATION WAS GIVEN:
WHEN	**WHERE**	**WHY** Joseph was working on the translation of the Bible and he had some questions about some of the things in the Book of Revelation. The Lord responded with this revelation.

Revelation 4:6-8

6 And before the throne there was a sea of glass like unto crystal: and in the midst of the throne, and round about the throne, were four beasts full of eyes before and behind.
7 And the first beast was like a lion, and the second beast like a calf, and the third beast had a face as a man, and the fourth beast was like a flying eagle.
8 And the four beasts had each of them six wings about him; and they were full of eyes within: and they rest not day and night, saying, Holy, holy, holy, Lord God Almighty, which was, and is, and is to come.

Revelation 4:4

4 And round about the throne were four and twenty seats: and upon the seats I saw four and twenty elders sitting, clothed in white raiment; and they had on their heads crowns of gold.

Revelation 5:1

1 And I saw in the right hand of him that sat on the throne a book written within and on the backside, sealed with seven seals.

Revelation 7:1-2

1 And after these things I saw four angels standing on the four corners of the earth, holding the four winds of the earth, that the wind should not blow on the earth, nor on the sea, nor on any tree.
2 And I saw another angel ascending from the east, having the seal of the living God: and he cried with a loud voice to the four angels, to whom it was given to hurt the earth and the sea,

Revelation 7:4-8

4 And I heard the number of them which were sealed: and there were sealed an hundred and forty and four thousand of all the tribes of the children of Israel.
5 Of the tribe of Juda were sealed twelve thousand. Of the tribe of Reuben were sealed twelve thousand. Of the tribe of Gad were sealed twelve thousand.
6 Of the tribe of Aser were sealed twelve thousand. Of the tribe of Nepthalim were sealed twelve thousand. Of the tribe of Manasses were sealed twelve thousand.
7 Of the tribe of Simeon were sealed twelve thousand. Of the tribe of Levi were sealed twelve thousand. Of the tribe of Issachar were sealed twelve thousand.
8 Of the tribe of Zabulon were sealed twelve thousand. Of the tribe of Joseph were sealed twelve thousand. Of the tribe of Benjamin were sealed twelve thousand.

Revelation 8:2 - 11:15

2 And I saw the seven angels which stood before God; and to them were given seven trumpets....

7 The first angel sounded, and there followed hail and fire mingled with blood, and they were cast upon the earth: and the third part of trees was burnt up, and all green grass was burnt up.

8 And the second angel sounded, and as it were a great mountain burning with fire was cast into the sea: and the third part of the sea became blood;...

10 And the third angel sounded, and there fell a great star from heaven, burning as it were a lamp, and it fell upon the third part of the rivers, and upon the fountains of waters;...

12 And the fourth angel sounded, and the third part of the sun was smitten, and the third part of the moon, and the third part of the stars; so as the third part of them was darkened, and the day shone not for a third part of it, and the night likewise....

1 And the fifth angel sounded, and I saw a star fall from heaven unto the earth: and to him was given the key of the bottomless pit....

9:13 And the sixth angel sounded, and I heard a voice from the four horns of the golden altar which is before God,...

11:15 And the seventh angel sounded; and there were great voices in heaven, saying, The kingdoms of this world are become the kingdoms of our Lord, and of his Christ; and he shall reign for ever and ever....

Revelation 10:10

10 And I took the little book out of the angel's hand, and ate it up; and it was in my mouth sweet as honey: and as soon as I had eaten it, my belly was bitter.

Revelation 11:3

3 And I will give power unto my two witnesses, and they shall prophesy a thousand two hundred and threescore days, clothed in sackcloth.

1	What is the sea of glass?	
2	What are we to understand by the four beasts?	
3	Are the four beasts limited to individual beasts, or do they represent classes or orders?	
4	What are we to understand by the eyes and wings, which the beasts had?	
5	What are we to understand by the four and twenty elders?	
6	What are we to understand by the book which John saw, which was sealed on the back with seven seals?	
7	What are we to understand by the seven seals with which it was sealed?	
8	What are we to understand by the four angels?	
9	What are we to understand by the angel ascending from the east?	
10	What time are the things spoken of in this chapter to be accomplished?	
11	What are we to understand by sealing the one hundred and forty-four thousand, out of all the tribes of Israel- twelve thousand out of every tribe?	
12	What are to understand by the sounding of the trumpets?	
13	When are the things to be accomplished which are written in the 9th chapter of Revelation?	
14	What are we to understand by the little book which was eaten by John?	
15	What is to be understood by the two witnesses?	

What does this section teach you about the principles of RECEIVING REVELATION and SCRIPTURE STUDY?

DOCTRINE & COVENANTS 78-80 TITLE:

78

WHEN	WHEN THIS REVELATION WAS GIVEN:	WHERE	WHERE THIS REVELATION WAS GIVEN:	WHY	WHAT WAS HAPPENING WHEN THIS REVELATION WAS GIVEN:

Study this section. As you study the verses below, record all of the doctrines and principles you can find in each verse's box. Include obvious ones and not-so-obvious doctrines and principles.

1-4 Organize a storehouse	5-8 Prepare yourselves for celestial world	9-12 Organize by a bond	13-14 That the Church may stand independent

15-16 Michael	17-18 I will lead you along	19-20 Receive all things with thankfulness	21-22 Every man his portion

79 TITLE:

WHEN	WHEN THIS REVELATION WAS GIVEN:	WHERE	WHERE THIS REVELATION WAS GIVEN:	WHY	WHAT WAS HAPPENING WHEN THIS REVELATION WAS GIVEN:

In your own words, what is this section about?

What are two phrases in this section that teach you a powerful principle? Write the phrase and your thoughts below.

1	2

80 TITLE:

WHEN	WHEN THIS REVELATION WAS GIVEN:	WHERE	WHERE THIS REVELATION WAS GIVEN:	WHY	WHAT WAS HAPPENING WHEN THIS REVELATION WAS GIVEN:

In your own words, what is this section about?

What are two phrases in this section that teach you a powerful principle? Write the phrase and your thoughts below.

1	2

81 TITLE:

WHEN THIS REVELATION WAS GIVEN:	WHERE THIS REVELATION WAS GIVEN:	WHAT WAS HAPPENING WHEN THIS REVELATION WAS GIVEN:
WHEN	WHERE	WHY

Study this section. As you study the verses below, record all of the doctrines and principles you can find in each verse's box. Include obvious ones and not-so-obvious doctrines and principles.

1-2 Keys of kingdom held by First Presidency	3-5 Requirement of counselor in First Presidency	4-6 Promise to counselor in First Presidency	7 The one who promises

* Note: at this time the Prophet and his counselors were called the "Presidency of the High Priesthood" (verse 2). Later they will be referred to as the First Presidency.

82 TITLE:

WHEN THIS REVELATION WAS GIVEN:	WHERE THIS REVELATION WAS GIVEN:	WHAT WAS HAPPENING WHEN THIS REVELATION WAS GIVEN:
WHEN	WHERE	WHY The Prophet and other brethren were now again in Missouri fulfilling the Lord's command to care for the poor. While there, he received this revelation.

Study this section. As you study the verses below, record all of the doctrines and principles you can find in each verse's box. Include obvious ones and not-so-obvious doctrines and principles.

1-4 Where much is given much is required	5-7 Darkness reigneth	8-10 The Lord is bound	11-14 Zion must increase
15-18 Must have equal claims	19 Seek interest of neighbor	20-21 An everlasting order	22-24 The kingdom is yours

83 TITLE:

WHEN THIS REVELATION WAS GIVEN:	WHERE THIS REVELATION WAS GIVEN:	WHAT WAS HAPPENING WHEN THIS REVELATION WAS GIVEN:
WHEN	WHERE	WHY

Study this section. As you study the verses below, record all of the doctrines and principles you can find in each verse's box. Include obvious ones and not-so-obvious doctrines and principles.

1-3 Women have claim on husbands for support	4 Children have claim on parents for support	5 Children can use storehouse when needed	6 Storehouse for widows and children

KEEP
COMMANDMENTS

THE LORD'S
PROMISES

I, the Lord, am bound when ye do what I say; but when ye do not what I say, ye have no promise.

DOCTRINE & COVENANTS 82:10

DOCTRINE & COVENANTS 82:10

THE LORD IS BOUND WHEN WE DO WHAT HE SAYS

"There are both moral and physical laws "irrevocably decreed in heaven before the foundations of this world" that cannot be changed. History demonstrates over and over again that moral standards cannot be changed by battle and cannot be changed by ballot. To legalize that which is basically wrong or evil will not prevent the pain and penalties that will follow as surely as night follows day."

PRESIDENT BOYD K. PACKER
October 2010 General Conference

1. What doctrines (truths) and principles can you find in this verse?

2. What principle did you find that can give you confidence as you strive to obey the Lord?

3. What are three experiences you have had that have shown you that this principle is true?

1-
2-
3-

4. What does this scripture teach you about the seminary doctrinal topic: "Ordinances and Covenants"?

TITLE:

WHEN THIS REVELATION WAS GIVEN:	WHERE THIS REVELATION WAS GIVEN:	WHAT WAS HAPPENING WHEN THIS REVELATION WAS GIVEN:
W H E N	W H E R E	W H Y

Study this section. As you study the verses below, record all of the doctrines and principles you can find in each verse's box. Include obvious ones and not-so-obvious doctrines and principles.

1-5 The New Jerusalem Temple	6-16 Line of Priesthood from Moses to Adam

6-16

Moses received the Holy Priesthood from J_____, who received it from C_____, who received it from E_____, who received it from J_____, who received it from G_____, who received it from E_____, who received it from _____.

Esaias lived in the days of A_____, who received the Priesthood from M_____, who received it through the lineage of his fathers, even till N_____, and Noah till E_____, through the lineage of their fathers. And from Enoch to A_____, who received the priesthood from A_____.

17 Priesthood in all generations	18 Aaronic Priesthood	19-22 The Melchizedek Priesthood	23-25 Origins of Aaronic Priesthood

26-28 Aaronic Priesthood keys	29-30 Priesthood offices	31-32 Priesthood shall be filled with glory	33-35 Oath & Covenant of Priesthood

36-39 Oath & Covenant of Priesthood	40-42 Oath & Covenant of Priesthood	43-45 Live by every word from God	46-47 The Spirit enlightens every man

48 The Priesthood benefits the whole world	49-53 How to recognize those in sin	54-57 Result of vanity & unbelief	58-62 Bear testimony and receive forgiveness

63-64 To the Apostles...	65-72 Signs that follow those who believe	73-75 Speak not these things before the world	76-79 I send you out...
80-82 Promises	83-85 Promises	86-90 He who receives you...	91-93 He who receives you not...
94-97 Warning for those who do not receive Christ	98-102 "The New Song"	103-105 Instructions	106-108 The ancient pattern
109-110 Everyone is needed	111-114 Responsibilities of offices	115-116 Promises	117-120 Go ye forth

What lessons and impressions did you receive about the Oath and Covenant of the Priesthood?

DOCTRINE & COVENANTS 84:20-22

THE POWER OF GODLINESS IS MANIFEST IN PRIESTHOOD ORDINANCES

20 Therefore, in the ordinances thereof, the power of godliness is manifest.

21 And without the ordinances thereof, and the authority of the priesthood, the power of godliness is not manifest unto men in the flesh;

22 For without this no man can see the face of God, even the Father, and live.

DOCTRINE & COVENANTS 84:20-22

"The temple is the object of every activity, every lesson, every progressive step in the Church. ... Ordinances of the temple are absolutely crucial. We cannot return to God's glory without them"

PRESIDENT RUSSELL M. NELSON
Ensign, Oct. 2010, 41

1. What doctrines (truths) and principles can you find in these verses?

2. What blessings can we receive through the priesthood?

3. What do you think the phrase "power of godliness" means?

4. What are some ordinances that are available to you (now and in the future)?

5. How do those ordinances offer you the power of godliness?

6. According to verse 22, why is it important for you to receive these ordinances?

7. What do these scriptures teach you about the seminary doctrinal topic: "Ordinances and Covenants"?

DOCTRINE & COVENANTS 85 TITLE:

WHEN THIS REVELATION WAS GIVEN:	WHERE THIS REVELATION WAS GIVEN:	WHAT WAS HAPPENING WHEN THIS REVELATION WAS GIVEN:
WHEN	WHERE	WHY Some Saints had moved to Zion in Missouri but had not consecrated their goods as had been commanded. Because of this, they could not receive inheritance. This revelation is a letter to W. W. Phelps giving instruction on this matter.

VERSES	DOCTRINES AND PRINCIPLES TAUGHT	WORDS LOOKED UP	INSIGHTS, THOUGHTS, LESSONS LEARNED
1			
2			
3			
4			
5			
6			
7			
8			
9			
10			
11			
12	**EZRA 2:61-62** 61 And of the children of the priests: the children of Habaiah, the children of Koz, the children of Barzillai; which took a wife of the daughters of Barzillai the Gileadite, and was called after their name: 62. These sought their register among those that were reckoned by genealogy, but they were not found: therefore were they, as polluted, put from the priesthood.		

TITLE:

	WHEN THIS REVELATION WAS GIVEN:	WHERE THIS REVELATION WAS GIVEN:	WHAT WAS HAPPENING WHEN THIS REVELATION WAS GIVEN:
WHEN		WHERE	WHY · This revelation was received as Joseph was working on the "JST" or the "Joseph Smith Translation of the Bible." This revelation gave clarification of the "Parable of the Wheat and the Tares" found in Matthew 13.

First: Read the parable that Joseph was reading in Matthew 13 (column 1).
Second: Write down questions you would ask the Lord about the parable (column 2).
Third: Read Doctrine & Covenants 86:1-7 and write what you learn about the parable. If one of your questions was answered, draw a line from your question to the answer (column3).
Fourth: In your own words, write what this parable is teaching and the lessons we can learn from it (column 4).

PARABLE	MY QUESTIONS	D&C 86:1-7	LESSONS LEARNED
MATTHEW 13:24-30 24 Another parable put he forth unto them, saying, The kingdom of heaven is likened unto a man which sowed good seed in his field: 25 But while men slept, his enemy came and sowed tares among the wheat, and went his way. 26 But when the blade was sprung up, and brought forth fruit, then appeared the tares also. 27 So the servants of the householder came and said unto him, Sir, didst not thou sow good seed in thy field? from whence then hath it tares? 28 He said unto them, An enemy hath done this. The servants said unto him, Wilt thou then that we go and gather them up? 29 But he said, Nay; lest while ye gather up the tares, ye root up also the wheat with them. 30 Let both grow together until the harvest: and in the time of harvest I will say to the reapers, Gather ye together first the tares, and bind them in bundles to burn them: but gather the wheat into my barn.		VERSES 1-2 VERSE 3 VERSE 4 VERSE 5 VERSE 6 VERSE 7	

The Role and Need for the Priesthood to Gather
What are some things you learn about the Priesthood in verses 8-11? Record what you find in the proper boxes.

86:8-9	86:10	86:11

DOCTRINE & COVENANTS 87 TITLE:

WHEN THIS REVELATION WAS GIVEN:	WHERE THIS REVELATION WAS GIVEN:	WHAT WAS HAPPENING WHEN THIS REVELATION WAS GIVEN:
WHEN	WHERE	WHY The United States Civil War began April 12, 1861 at Fort Sumter, South Carolina, 29 years after this revelation was received and 17 years after Joseph Smith had died. Joseph and the brethren were aware of the growing conflict over slavery and were pondering upon the subject of slavery in the United States and throughout the world.

VERSES	DOCTRINES AND PRINCIPLES TAUGHT	WORDS LOOKED UP	INSIGHTS, THOUGHTS, LESSONS LEARNED
1			
2			
3			
4			
5			
6			
7			
8			

TITLE:

WHEN THIS REVELATION WAS GIVEN:	WHERE THIS REVELATION WAS GIVEN:	WHAT WAS HAPPENING WHEN THIS REVELATION WAS GIVEN:
WHEN	**WHERE**	**WHY** Knowing what was soon coming in the United States, the brethren were anxious to know the Lord's will concerning the building of Zion. They held a conference and the Lord's Spirit was poured upon them. This section contains powerful doctrine that gave peace to their hearts. Joseph called this revelation the "olive leaf... the Lord's message of peace to us."

VERSES	DOCTRINES AND PRINCIPLES TAUGHT	WORDS LOOKED UP	INSIGHTS, THOUGHTS, LESSONS LEARNED
1-2			
3-5			
6-7			
8-10			
11-13			
14-17			
18-20	*Note: "It" in these verses refers to the earth (from verse 17)		
21-24			
25-26			
27-29			
30-31			
32-33			
34-36			

VERSES	DOCTRINES AND PRINCIPLES TAUGHT	WORDS LOOKED UP	INSIGHTS, THOUGHTS, LESSONS LEARNED
37-39			
40			
41-43			
44-45			
46-48			
49-50			
51-61			
62-65			
66-68			
69-73			
74-76			
77-80			
81-85			

VERSES	DOCTRINES AND PRINCIPLES TAUGHT	WORDS LOOKED UP	INSIGHTS, THOUGHTS, LESSONS LEARNED
86-88		104	
89-91			
92-94			
95-96			
97-98			
99-100			
101-103			
104-105			
106-107			
108-110			
111-113			
114-116			
117-119			
120-121			

VERSES	DOCTRINES AND PRINCIPLES TAUGHT	WORDS LOOKED UP	INSIGHTS, THOUGHTS, LESSONS LEARNED
122-123			
124-126			
127-128			
129-131			
132-133			
134-135			
136-137			
138-139			
140-141			

Lessons WHAT ARE SOME OF THE MOST IMPORTANT LESSONS YOU CAN LEARN FROM THIS SECTION?

DOCTRINE & COVENANTS 88:118

SEEK LEARNING BY STUDY AND FAITH

And as all have not faith, seek ye diligently and teach one another words of wisdom; yea, seek ye out of the best books words of wisdom; seek learning, even by study and also by faith.

DOCTRINE & COVENANTS 88:118

""Learning by faith requires spiritual, mental, and physical exertion and not just passive reception. ...

"... Learning by faith cannot be transferred from an instructor to a student through a lecture, a demonstration, or an experiential exercise; rather, a student must exercise faith and act in order to obtain the knowledge for himself or herself."

ELDER DAVID A. BEDNAR
Ensign, Sept. 2007, 64

1. What doctrines (truths) and principles can you find in this verse?

2. This revelation was given to the members of the School of the Prophets. How were these brethren to seek learning?

3. What do you think it means to learn "by study and also by faith"?

4. What do you learn about this principle from Elder Bednar's quote at the top of the page?

5. Why is acting on what you learn an important part of learning?

6. What are some times in your life you have been an example of this verse?

7. What does this scripture teach you about the seminary doctrinal topic: "Acquiring Spiritual Knowledge"?

DOCTRINE & COVENANTS 89 TITLE:

WHEN THIS REVELATION WAS GIVEN:	WHERE THIS REVELATION WAS GIVEN:	WHAT WAS HAPPENING WHEN THIS REVELATION WAS GIVEN:
WHEN	WHERE	WHY

Study this section. As you study the verses below, record all of the doctrines and principles you can find in each verse's box. Include obvious ones and not-so-obvious doctrines and principles.

1-2 Word of Wisdom	3 Principle with promise	4 Forewarning	5 Wine & strong drink
6 Sacrament wine	**7** Use of strong drinks	**8** Tobacco	**9** Hot drinks
10 Herbs	**11** Fruit	**12** Flesh of beasts	**13** Flesh of beasts
14 Grain	**15** Grain	**16** Grain	**17** Grain
18 Promise	**19** Promise	**20** Promise	**21** Promise

DOCTRINE & COVENANTS 89:18-21

BLESSINGS OF THE WORD OF WISDOM

18 And all saints who remember to keep and do these sayings, walking in obedience to the commandments, shall receive health in their navel and marrow to their bones;
19 And shall find wisdom and great treasures of knowledge, even hidden treasures;
20 And shall run and not be weary, and shall walk and not faint.
21 And I, the Lord, give unto them a promise, that the destroying angel shall pass by them, as the children of Israel, and not slay them. Amen.

DOCTRINE & COVENANTS 89:18-21

"I have come to know … that a fundamental purpose of the Word of Wisdom has to do with revelation. …

"If someone 'under the influence' can hardly listen to plain talk, how can they respond to spiritual promptings that touch their most delicate feelings?

"As valuable as the Word of Wisdom is as a law of health, it may be much more valuable to you spiritually than it is physically"

PRESIDENT BOYD K. PACKER
Ensign, Nov. 1979, 20

1. What blessings does the Lord promise to those who keep the Word of Wisdom?

PROMISES IN VERSE 18:	
PROMISES IN VERSE 19:	
PROMISES IN VERSE 20:	
PROMISES IN VERSE 21:	

2. How can observing the Word of Wisdom help us obtain wisdom and knowledge? (See President Boyd K. Packer's quote above)

3. When have you seen the promises in these scriptures fulfilled in your life or the life of someone you know?

4. As times move forward and Satan provides new ways for us to destroy our bodies, prophets continue to give us modern information to help us receive all the blessings from the Word of Wisdom. Look up "Physical and Emotional Health" in *For the Strength of Youth* and fill this space with phrases that stand out to you.

5. What do these scriptures teach you about the seminary doctrinal topic: "Commandments"?

90

WHEN	WHEN THIS REVELATION WAS GIVEN:	WHERE	WHERE THIS REVELATION WAS GIVEN:	WHY	WHAT WAS HAPPENING WHEN THIS REVELATION WAS GIVEN:

VERSES	DOCTRINES AND PRINCIPLES TAUGHT	WORDS LOOKED UP	INSIGHTS, THOUGHTS, LESSONS LEARNED
1-3			
4-7			
8-11			
12-15			
16-20			
21-25			
26-29			
30-33			
34-37			

91 TITLE:

WHEN	WHEN THIS REVELATION WAS GIVEN:	WHERE	WHERE THIS REVELATION WAS GIVEN:	WHY	WHAT WAS HAPPENING WHEN THIS REVELATION WAS GIVEN:

Look up "Apocrypha" in the Bible Dictionary. Give a description of what it is here:

When Joseph Smith asked the Lord if he should translate the Apocrypha, what was the Lord's answer? (vs. 1-6)

92 TITLE:

WHEN	WHEN THIS REVELATION WAS GIVEN:	WHERE	WHERE THIS REVELATION WAS GIVEN:	WHY	WHAT WAS HAPPENING WHEN THIS REVELATION WAS GIVEN:

What instructions did the Lord give to Frederick G. Williams in this section?

TITLE:

WHEN THIS REVELATION WAS GIVEN:	WHERE THIS REVELATION WAS GIVEN:	WHAT WAS HAPPENING WHEN THIS REVELATION WAS GIVEN
WHEN	**WHERE**	This was a time of trials for the Saints. In Ohio, many were leaving the Church and becoming apostates; and in Missouri, mobs were persecuting the Saints. This revelation gave them great instruction and peace.

Study this section. As you study the verses below, record all of the doctrines and principles you can find in each verse's box. Include obvious ones and not-so-obvious doctrines and principles.

(1-5) The Father and the Son	(6-9) John's record	(10-14) John's record	(15-18) John's record
(19-20) We receive grace for grace until fulness	(21-22) Church of the Firstborn	(23-24) Truth	(25) Truth
(26-28) How to receive a fulness of truth	(29-31) Truth is independent	(32-35) Fulness of joy at resurrection	(36-37) Glory of God is light and truth
(38-39) Wicked one taketh away light and truth	(40-44) Bring your children up in light and truth	(45-46) Friends and servants	(47-48) Rebuked before the Lord
(49) Pray always	(50) Set in order family	(51-52) Make haste	(53) Translate and obtain a knowledge

DOCTRINE & COVENANTS 94-96

94 TITLE:

WHEN THIS REVELATION WAS GIVEN:	WHERE THIS REVELATION WAS GIVEN:	WHAT WAS HAPPENING WHEN THIS REVELATION WAS GIVEN:
WHEN	WHERE	WHY The Saints had been purchasing land in Kirtland and once they had obtained a large portion, the Lord told them in what manner to build the city. The plan was similar to the city plans revealed to them for Missouri.

VERSES	INSTRUCTIONS FOR KIRTLAND
1-2	
3-9	
10-12	
13-17	

95 TITLE:

WHEN THIS REVELATION WAS GIVEN:	WHERE THIS REVELATION WAS GIVEN:	WHAT WAS HAPPENING WHEN THIS REVELATION WAS GIVEN:
WHEN	WHERE	WHY The Saints had been commanded to build the temple in Kirtland 6 months before (see D&C 88:119), but they were poor and had delayed the construction. The Lord then gave them this revelation.

VERSES	DOCTRINES AND PRINCIPLES TAUGHT	WORDS LOOKED UP	INSIGHTS, THOUGHTS, LESSONS LEARNED
1-2			
3-4			
5-6			
7-8			
9-10			
11-12			
13-15			
16-17			

96 TITLE:

WHEN THIS REVELATION WAS GIVEN:	WHERE THIS REVELATION WAS GIVEN:	WHAT WAS HAPPENING WHEN THIS REVELATION WAS GIVEN:
WHEN	WHERE	WHY The location for the Kirtland Temple was to be located on "the French Farm." They could not decide who would oversee that land and how the rest of the farm should be divided. This revelation followed.

VERSES	INSTRUCTIONS FOR KIRTLAND
1	
2-5	
6-9	

TITLE:

WHEN THIS REVELATION WAS GIVEN:	WHERE THIS REVELATION WAS GIVEN:	WHAT WAS HAPPENING WHEN THIS REVELATION WAS GIVEN:
WHEN	WHERE	The Saints in Missouri began to be under severe persecution. A mob destroyed W. W. Phelp's printing press, Saints were turned out of their homes, and Edward Partridge and Charles Allen were tarred and feathered. Joseph, unaware of the seriousness of the situation, sent them this revelation in a letter (section 98 was included as well).

VERSES	DOCTRINES, INSTRUCTIONS, AND PRINCIPLES TAUGHT	WORDS LOOKED UP	INSIGHTS, THOUGHTS, LESSONS LEARNED
1-2			
3-5			
6-7			
8-9			
10-12			
13-14			
15-17			
18-19			
20-21			
22-24			
25-26			
27-28			

DOCTRINE & COVENANTS 98 TITLE:

	WHEN THIS REVELATION WAS GIVEN:	WHERE THIS REVELATION WAS GIVEN:	WHAT WAS HAPPENING WHEN THIS REVELATION WAS GIVEN:
WHEN		WHERE	WHY

VERSES	DOCTRINES, INSTRUCTIONS, AND PRINCIPLES TAUGHT	WORDS LOOKED UP	INSIGHTS, THOUGHTS, LESSONS LEARNED
1-3			
4-8			
9-10			
11-12			
13-15			
16-18			
19-22			
23-31			
32-38			
39-40			
41-44			
45-48			

99 TITLE:

WHEN THIS REVELATION WAS GIVEN:	WHERE THIS REVELATION WAS GIVEN:	WHAT WAS HAPPENING WHEN THIS REVELATION WAS GIVEN:
WHEN	WHERE	This revelation is the call for John Murdock to serve a mission in the Eastern States.

INSTRUCTION, PROMISES, AND TEACHINGS GIVEN TO JOHN MURDOCK

Verse 1

Verse 2

Verse 3

Verse 4

Verse 5

Verse 6

Verse 7

Verse 8

100 TITLE:

WHEN THIS REVELATION WAS GIVEN:	WHERE THIS REVELATION WAS GIVEN:	WHAT WAS HAPPENING WHEN THIS REVELATION WAS GIVEN:
WHEN	WHERE	Joseph and Sidney were on a mission that went as far as Canada. While Joseph was on his mission, he felt great anxiety for his family and received this revelation to comfort him.

INSTRUCTION, PROMISES, AND TEACHINGS GIVEN TO JOHN MURDOCK

Verses 1-2

Verses 3-4

Verses 5-6

Verses 7-8

Verses 9-10

Verses 11-12

Verses 13-14

Verse 15

Verses 16-17

DOCTRINE & COVENANTS 101   TITLE:

WHEN	WHEN THIS REVELATION WAS GIVEN:	WHERE	WHERE THIS REVELATION WAS GIVEN:	WHY	WHAT WAS HAPPENING WHEN THIS REVELATION WAS GIVEN:

Study this section. As you study the verses below, record all of the doctrines and principles you can find in each verse's box. Include obvious ones and not-so-obvious doctrines and principles.

1-5 Purpose of persecution	6-8 The transgressions	9-11 "I will remember mercy"	12-16 Those found upon the watch-tower

17-22 "They shall be called stakes"	23-24 The Second Coming	25-35 Life during the Millennium

*List all of the things you learn about life during the Millennium

36-38 Care for the soul	39-42 Salt of the earth	43-62 Parable of the Nobleman and the Olive Trees

Verses	What is happening in the parable	What I think this means
43-45		
46		
47-49		
50		
51		
52-54		
55-58		
59-62		

63-67 All the churches	68-73 Do not gather in haste

74-75 Continue to gather	76-80 The Lord established the Constitution of the United States

Verses	What is happening in the parable
81-82	
83	
84	
85	
86-88	
89-91	
92	

CHILDREN OF ISRAEL

(93-95) That their ears may be opened	(96-97) "Let not that which I have appointed be polluted"	(98-99) A very sore and grievous sin	(100-101) They shall dwell thereon

Lessons

WHAT ARE SOME OF THE MOST IMPORTANT LESSONS YOU CAN LEARN FROM THIS SECTION?

DOCTRINE & COVENANTS 102 TITLE:

WHEN	WHEN THIS REVELATION WAS GIVEN:	WHERE	WHERE THIS REVELATION WAS GIVEN:	WHY	WHAT WAS HAPPENING WHEN THIS REVELATION WAS GIVEN:
					As missionary efforts moved forward, the Saints now numbered over 3000 members. With so many Saints, there was a need for more leadership and organization. The first high council was formed on February 17, 1834. Orson Hyde noticed that there were errors in the minutes (meeting's notes). Joseph made inspired corrections the following day.

VERSES	DOCTRINES, INSTRUCTIONS, AND PRINCIPLES TAUGHT	WORDS LOOKED UP	INSIGHTS, THOUGHTS, LESSONS LEARNED
1-2			

3

PRESIDENTS		MEMBERS OF THE FIRST HIGH COUNCIL IN THIS DISPENSATION			
1-	1-	4-	7-	10-	
2-	2-	5-	8-	11-	
3-	3-	6-	9-	12-	

VERSES			
4			
5-8			
9-11			
12-14			
15-17			
18-19			
20-23			
24-27			
28-31			
32-34			

DOCTRINE & COVENANTS 103 TITLE:

WHEN WHEN THIS REVELATION WAS GIVEN:	WHERE WHERE THIS REVELATION WAS GIVEN:	WHAT WAS HAPPENING WHEN THIS REVELATION WAS GIVEN:
		As the Saints in Missouri were still displaced from their homes and under severe persecution, the brethren sought counsel on how they could assist the Saints. The revelation was received where they were instructed to gather people and resources and travel to Zion. This group was later known as "Zion's Camp."

1-4 Why the Lord allowed this to happen	5-8 How to prevail	9-10 Salt	11-13 Redemption of Zion
14-15 Redemption of Zion	16-18 Redemption of Zion	19-20 Redemption of Zion	21-23 Gather unto Zion
24-26 "My presence shall be with you"	27-28 Lay down life	29-30 Organization of Zion's Camp	31-34 Organization of Zion's Camp
35 Organization of Zion's Camp	36 How victory and glory comes to pass	37-40 Organization of Zion's Camp	

WHEN	WHEN THIS REVELATION WAS GIVEN:	WHERE	WHERE THIS REVELATION WAS GIVEN:	WHY	WHAT WAS HAPPENING WHEN THIS REVELATION WAS GIVEN:

1-2 Immutable promises of the United Order	3-5 Consequence of covetousness & feigned words	6-10 Transgressors of the order	11-13 Stewards over earthly blessings

14-18 The Lord's way of providing	19-46 Stewardships of various men

19-23   Sidney Rigdon :

24-26   Martin Harris :

27,29-33 Frederick G. Williams :

28-33   Oliver Cowdery :

34-38   John Johnson :

39-42   Newel K. Whitney :

43-46   Joseph Smith Jr. :

47-53 Kirtland and Zion to have separate United Orders	54-59 Printing of the scriptures	60-66 A treasury	67-73 Another treasury

74-75 Who can take part	76-77 The treasurer	78-80 How to be delivered from financial bondage	81-86 How to be delivered from financial bondage

TITLE:

WHEN THIS REVELATION WAS GIVEN:	WHERE THIS REVELATION WAS GIVEN:	WHAT WAS HAPPENING WHEN THIS REVELATION WAS GIVEN:
WHEN	WHERE	Joseph and 200 others had formed Zion's Camp and had marched 1,000 miles to assist the Saints who had been displaced from their homes and were under constant threat of mob violence. They had left on May 4th. Now, seven weeks later, they were close to Liberty, Missouri (their destination) and become aware of mobs planning to attack. They camped on a hill between two branches of Fishing River and were approached by armed men who delivered the message that they would "see hell before morning" and 400 men were coming to destroy them. As they prepared for battle, a cloud appeared and a fierce storm arrived as some of the mob was crossing the river. The storm was so terrible that it destroyed crops and soaked their ammunition, preventing them to attack. Three days later, while still camping on Fishing River, Joseph received this revelation.

Record what Joseph learned about Zion and Zion's Camp in this revelation.

What lessons can I learn from these verses?

HOW ZION SHALL BE BUILT 1-5		
WAIT FOR A LITTLE SEASON 6-13		
I WILL FIGHT YOUR BATTLES 14-19		
WISE COUNSEL 20-30		
BLESSINGS THAT AWAIT 31-37		
LIFT AN ENSIGN OF PEACE 38-41		

WHEN THIS REVELATION WAS GIVEN:	WHERE THIS REVELATION WAS GIVEN:	WHAT WAS HAPPENING WHEN THIS REVELATION WAS GIVEN:
WHEN	WHERE	WHY This revelation is directed towards Oliver Cowdery's older brother, Warren Cowdery. Due to preaching and missionary work, a branch was established in Freedom, New York. Warren is called to preside over this branch.

Verses	Instructions given to Warren A. Cowdery	Doctrine and Principles taught	Lessons I learn from these verses
1-2			
3			
4-5			
6			
7			
8			

TITLE:

WHEN	WHERE	WHY
WHEN THIS REVELATION WAS GIVEN:	WHERE THIS REVELATION WAS GIVEN:	WHAT WAS HAPPENING WHEN THIS REVELATION WAS GIVEN:

(1) Two Priesthoods	(2-4) Name of Melchizedek Priesthood	(5) Appendages	(6-9) The Melchizedek Priesthood
(10-12) The Melchizedek Priesthood	(13-14) Name of Aaronic Priesthood	(15-17) The Aaronic Priesthood	(18-19) The Melchizedek Priesthood
(20) The Aaronic Priesthood	(21) Officers	(22-24) Quorums of Twelve and Seventy	(25-26) Quorums of Twelve and Seventy
(27-32) Decisions in Quorums	(33-35) Responsibilities of Twelve & Seventy	(36-37) Stake High Councils	(38-39) Duty of Councils

40-41 Order of the Priesthood	42-52 Patriarchal Order
	Record what you learn about each of these men.

Seth 42-43	Enos 44	Cainan 45	Mahalaleel 46	Jared 47
Enoch 48-49	Methuselah 50	Lamech 51	Noah 52	Adam 42-50

53-57 Adam and his posterity in Adam-ondi-Ahman	58-63 Officers of Church in order	64-67 Officers of Church in order	68-73 Office of Bishop

74-76 Office of Bishop	77-81 First Presidency and Twelve are highest court	82-84 None exempt from justice	85-89 Numbers in each quorum

90 Elder's quorum presidency	91-92 President of Church	93-97 Presidents of Seventy	98 Who travels and who does not

99 Learn your duty	100 He that is slothful		

DOCTRINE & COVENANTS 107:8

THE AUTHORITY OF THE MELCHIZEDEK PRIESTHOOD

The Melchizedek Priesthood holds the right of presidency, and has power and authority over all the offices in the church in all ages of the world, to administer in spiritual things.

DOCTRINE & COVENANTS 107:8

"When priesthood authority is exercised properly, priesthood bearers do what He [Jesus Christ] would do if He were present."

PRESIDENT BOYD K. PACKER
April 2010 General Conference

1. What doctrines (truths) and principles can you find in this verse?

2. What right and authority does the Melchizedek Priesthood hold?

3. "Administer[ing] in spiritual things" includes administering blessings, ordinances, and covenants. Make a list of times you have had spiritual things administered unto you by the Melchizedek Priesthood.

4. During which time periods upon the earth has the Melchizedek Priesthood held these rights and authority?

5. Look up "Melchizedek Priesthood" in *True to the Faith* and answer the questions below. If you do not have a *True to the Faith* book, you can find it on the "Gospel Library App" under "Youth," or you can search "True to the Faith" on lds.org.

   - What are the names of the two priesthoods?

   - Why is the Melchizedek Priesthood considered "greater"?

   - Who was the first man on earth to receive the Melchizedek Priesthood?

   - What are the offices in the Melchizedek Priesthood?

6. What does this scripture teach you about the seminary doctrinal topic: "Priesthood and Priesthood Keys"?

DOCTRINE & COVENANTS 108 TITLE:

Verses	Instructions given to Lyman Sherman	Doctrine and Principles taught	Lessons I learn from these verses
1-2			
3			
4-5			
6			
7			
8			

TITLE:

WHEN THIS REVELATION WAS GIVEN:	WHERE THIS REVELATION WAS GIVEN:	WHAT WAS HAPPENING WHEN THIS REVELATION WAS GIVEN:
WHEN	WHERE	After three years, the Saints finished building the Kirtland Temple. The Lord revealed the dedicatory prayer to Joseph Smith. This revelation is that prayer.

VERSES	DOCTRINES, INSTRUCTIONS AND PRINCIPLES TAUGHT	WORDS LOOKED UP	WHAT THIS TEACHES ME ABOUT TEMPLES
1-5			
6-8			
9-12			
13-15			
16-19			
20-23			
24-27			
28-31			
32-35			
36-38			
39-41			
42-44			

VERSES	DOCTRINES AND PRINCIPLES TAUGHT	WORDS LOOKED UP	WHAT THIS TEACHES ME ABOUT TEMPLES
45-47			
48-50			
51-53			
54-57			
58-61			
62-64			
65-67			
68-70			
71-72			
73-74			
75-76			
77-78			
79-80			

WHEN THIS REVELATION WAS GIVEN:	WHERE THIS REVELATION WAS GIVEN:	WHAT WAS HAPPENING WHEN THIS REVELATION WAS GIVEN:
W H E N	W H E R E	Shortly after the Kirtland Temple was dedicated, the Saints held a sacrament meeting in the temple. Joseph and Oliver went to a part of the temple where a veil separated them from the rest of the congregation. In that place, Jesus Christ and others appeared to them.

Record what is happening and being taught in these verses.   What lessons can I learn from these verses?

They see the Lord, Jesus Christ 1-6		
The Lord accepts the temple 7-10		
Moses appears 11		
Elias appears 12		
Elijah appears 13-16		

DOCTRINE & COVENANTS 111-112

WHEN	WHEN THIS REVELATION WAS GIVEN:	WHERE	WHERE THIS REVELATION WAS GIVEN:	WHY	WHAT WAS HAPPENING WHEN THIS REVELATION WAS GIVEN:

VERSES	DOCTRINES AND PRINCIPLES TAUGHT	WORDS LOOKED UP	INSIGHTS, THOUGHTS, LESSONS LEARNED
1-3			
4-5			
6-8			
9-10			
11			

112 TITLE:

WHEN	WHEN THIS REVELATION WAS GIVEN:	WHERE	WHERE THIS REVELATION WAS GIVEN:	WHY	WHAT WAS HAPPENING WHEN THIS REVELATION WAS GIVEN:

VERSES	DOCTRINES AND PRINCIPLES TAUGHT	WORDS LOOKED UP	INSIGHTS, THOUGHTS, LESSONS LEARNED
1-3			
4-7			
8-10			
11-15			
16-20			
21-25			
26-29			
30-34			

TITLE:

WHEN	WHEN THIS REVELATION WAS GIVEN:	WHERE	WHERE THIS REVELATION WAS GIVEN:	WHY	WHAT WAS HAPPENING WHEN THIS REVELATION WAS GIVEN:

1. Read the scripture in Isaiah	2. Write down the questions you have	3. Write down the question Joseph asked the Lord	4. Write down the answer Joseph received	5. Record the insights you gain

VERSES 1-2

ISAIAH 11:1

And there shall come forth a rod out of the stem of Jesse, and a Branch shall grow out of his roots:

VERSES 3-4

ISAIAH 11:1

And there shall come forth a rod out of the stem of Jesse, and a Branch shall grow out of his roots:

VERSES 5-6

ISAIAH 11:10

And in that day there shall be a root of Jesse, which shall stand for an ensign of the people; to it shall the Gentiles seek: and his rest shall be glorious.

VERSES 7-8

ISAIAH 52:1

Awake, awake; put on thy strength, O Zion; put on thy beautiful garments, O Jerusalem, The holy city: for henceforth there shall no more come into thee the uncircumcised and the unclean.

VERSES 9-10

ISAIAH 52:2

Shake thyself from the dust; arise, and sit down, O Jerusalem: loose thyself from the bands of thy neck, O captive daughter of Zion

DOCTRINE & COVENANTS 114-116

114 TITLE:

WHEN THIS REVELATION WAS GIVEN:	WHERE THIS REVELATION WAS GIVEN:	WHAT WAS HAPPENING WHEN THIS REVELATION WAS GIVEN:
WHEN	**WHERE**	**WHY**

What important principles can you see in this revelation?

115 TITLE:

WHEN THIS REVELATION WAS GIVEN:	WHERE THIS REVELATION WAS GIVEN:	WHAT WAS HAPPENING WHEN THIS REVELATION WAS GIVEN:
WHEN	**WHERE**	**WHY** In this revelation, Jesus Christ names His church.

VERSES	DOCTRINES AND PRINCIPLES TAUGHT	WORDS LOOKED UP	INSIGHTS, THOUGHTS, LESSONS LEARNED
1-4			
5-6			
7-12			
13-16			
17-19			

116 TITLE:

WHEN THIS REVELATION WAS GIVEN:	WHERE THIS REVELATION WAS GIVEN:	WHAT WAS HAPPENING WHEN THIS REVELATION WAS GIVEN:
WHEN	**WHERE**	**WHY** In this revelation, Joseph receives revelation on the location of Adam-ondi-Ahman (see D&C 107:53-57). This location has ancient significance as well as future importance.

What do you learn about Adam-ondi-Ahman in this revelation?

117 TITLE:

WHEN THIS REVELATION WAS GIVEN:	WHERE THIS REVELATION WAS GIVEN:	WHAT WAS HAPPENING WHEN THIS REVELATION WAS GIVEN:
W H E N	W H E R E	Joseph received this and the following three revelations while in Far West, Missouri. In this section, note the instructions that William Marks, Newel K. Whitney, and Oliver Granger received.

VERSES	INSTRUCTIONS AND TEACHINGS GIVEN WILLIAM, NEWEL, & OLIVER	INSIGHTS, THOUGHTS, LESSONS LEARNED
1-3		
4-5		
6-9		
10-13		
14-16		

118 TITLE:

WHEN THIS REVELATION WAS GIVEN:	WHERE THIS REVELATION WAS GIVEN:	WHAT WAS HAPPENING WHEN THIS REVELATION WAS GIVEN:
W H E N	W H E R E	Kirtland went through a period of Apostasy and some of the Twelve Apostles had fallen away. This section reveals the replacements for those men.

VERSES	INSTRUCTIONS AND TEACHINGS GIVEN	INSIGHTS, THOUGHTS, LESSONS LEARNED
1-2		
3		
4-6		

DOCTRINE & COVENANTS 119-120

119 TITLE:

WHEN	WHEN THIS REVELATION WAS GIVEN:	WHERE	WHERE THIS REVELATION WAS GIVEN:	WHY	WHAT WAS HAPPENING WHEN THIS REVELATION WAS GIVEN:

VERSES	DOCTRINES AND PRINCIPLES TAUGHT	WORDS LOOKED UP	INSIGHTS, THOUGHTS, LESSONS LEARNED
1-2			
3			
4			
5			
6-7			

120 TITLE:

WHEN	WHEN THIS REVELATION WAS GIVEN:	WHERE	WHERE THIS REVELATION WAS GIVEN:	WHY	WHAT WAS HAPPENING WHEN THIS REVELATION WAS GIVEN:
					In the previous section, the Lord revealed the Law of Tithing. In this section, He revealed whose responsibility it was to dispose of the tithing, or rather, whose responsibility it was to properly handle the tithing received.

What important doctrines and principles do you learn from this section (use the footnotes)?

WHEN THIS REVELATION WAS GIVEN:	WHERE THIS REVELATION WAS GIVEN:	WHAT WAS HAPPENING WHEN THIS REVELATION WAS GIVEN:
WHEN	WHERE	On October 27, 1838 the Governor of Missouri, Governor Boggs, gave what is now known as "the extermination order." This order proclaimed the Mormons as enemies and that they needed to be exterminated or driven from the state. Shortly after, Joseph and 5 others (Hyrum Smith, Lyman Wight, Caleb Baldwin, Alexander McRae, and Sidney Rigdon) were arrested on false charges and held in jail for several months. The jail conditions were miserable. Some have nicknamed this jail as a "Temple Prison" as Joseph prophesied from there and sent the Church a letter filled with glorious teachings. Sections 121, 122, and 123 are these letters.

	VERSES	DOCTRINES AND PRINCIPLES TAUGHT	WORDS LOOKED UP	THOUGHTS, INSIGHTS, & LESSONS LEARNED
THE QUESTIONS	1-3			
	4-6			
THE ANSWERS	7-8			
	9-11			
	12-14			
	15-17			
	18-20			
	21-23			
	24-27			
	28-30			
	31-32			
	33			

VERSES	DOCTRINES AND PRINCIPLES TAUGHT	WORDS LOOKED UP	THOUGHTS, INSIGHTS, & LESSONS LEARNED
34-35			
36			
37-38			
39			
40			
41			
42			
43-44			
45			
46			

DOCTRINE OF THE PRIESTHOOD

36 That the rights of the priesthood are insepara-bly connected with the powers of heaven, and that the powers of heaven cannot be controlled nor handled only upon the principles of righteous-ness....

41 No power or influence can or ought to be maintained by virtue of the priesthood, only by persuasion, by long-suffering, by gentleness and meekness, and by love unfeigned;

42 By kindness, and pure knowledge, which shall greatly enlarge the soul without hypocrisy, and without guile—

DOCTRINE & COVENANTS 121:36, 41-42

DOCTRINE & COVENANTS 121:36, 41-42

PRIESTHOOD POWER DEPENDS ON ONE'S RIGHTEOUSNESS

The power of the priesthood is God's power operating through men and boys like us and requires personal righteousness, faithfulness, obedience, and diligence. A boy or a man may receive priesthood authority by the laying on of hands but will have no priesthood power if he is disobedient, unworthy, or unwilling to serve. …

"… Priesthood holders young and old need both authority and power—the necessary permission and the spiritual capacity to represent God in the work of salvation."

ELDER DAVID A. BEDNAR
April 2012 General Conference

1. A man receives the right to exercise the priesthood when priesthood authority is conferred upon him by the laying on of hands. According to verse 36, even though a man may have the rights of the priesthood, what must he be in order to draw upon the powers of heaven?

2. According to verses 41 and 42, what are some attitudes and actions that help priesthood holders draw on the powers of heaven to help other people? Fill in the words below in the left column. In the center column, write what you think they mean. In the right column, write the name of a priesthood holder in your life who is a good example of that attitude or action.

ATTITUDE / ACTION	WHAT IT MEANS	EXAMPLE
P		
L		
G		
M		
L		
K		
P		

3. What do these scriptures teach you about the seminary doctrinal topic: "Priesthood and Priesthood Keys"?

DOCTRINE & COVENANTS 122 TITLE:

VERSES	DOCTRINES AND PRINCIPLES TAUGHT	WORDS LOOKED UP	THOUGHTS, INSIGHTS, & LESSONS LEARNED
1			
2-3			
4			
5			
6			
7			
8			
9			

TITLE:

WHEN	WHEN THIS REVELATION WAS GIVEN:	WHERE	WHERE THIS REVELATION WAS GIVEN:	WHY	WHAT WAS HAPPENING WHEN THIS REVELATION WAS GIVEN:

VERSES	DOCTRINES AND PRINCIPLES TAUGHT	WORDS LOOKED UP	THOUGHTS, INSIGHTS, & LESSONS LEARNED
1-3			
4-5			
6			
7			
8-10			
11-12			
13-14			
15-17			

DOCTRINE & COVENANTS 124 TITLE:

WHEN THIS REVELATION WAS GIVEN:	WHERE THIS REVELATION WAS GIVEN:	WHAT WAS HAPPENING WHEN THIS REVELATION WAS GIVEN:
WHEN	**WHERE**	**WHY** Much has come to pass since the last revelation. The Saints were now in Nauvoo and had been there for two years; 3000 Saints lived there and they were about to build a temple. This is the first revelation received there that was included in the Doctrine & Covenants.

(1) Joseph's purpose	(2-5) "make a solemn proclamation"	(6-9) "make a solemn proclamation"	(10-14) "make a solemn proclamation"
(15-17) Blessed men	(18-21) Blessed men	(22-28) Build a boarding house for strangers	(29-31) Baptisms for the dead
(32-34) Baptisms for the dead	(35-36) Baptisms for the dead	(37-39) Temples built for ordinances	(40-44) Temples built for ordinances
(45-48) Polluted holy grounds	(49-51) Enemies hindering the work	(52-55) Consequences upon Missouri	(56-61) The boarding house / Nauvoo House

(62-81) Stock in the Nauvoo House	(82-91) William Law	(91-93) Hyrum Smith becomes Patriarch	(94-96) Hyrum Smith becomes Patriarch
(97-99) Counsel to William Law	(100-102) Counsel to William Law	(103-110) Counsel to Sidney Rigdon	(111-114) Counsel to Amos Davies
(115-118) Counsel to Robert D. Foster	(119-122) Nauvoo House stock requirements	(123-126) Officers named with duties & quorums	(127-130) Officers named with duties & quorums
(131-135) Officers named with duties & quorums	(136-139) Officers named with duties & quorums	(140) Difference in quorums	(141-142) Officers named with duties & quorums
(143) Purpose of offices	(144-145) Fill these offices		

DOCTRINE & COVENANTS 125-126

125 TITLE:

WHEN THIS REVELATION WAS GIVEN:	WHERE THIS REVELATION WAS GIVEN:	WHAT WAS HAPPENING WHEN THIS REVELATION WAS GIVEN:
WHEN	WHERE	WHY

VERSES	INSTRUCTIONS & TEACHINGS GIVEN
1	
2	
3	
4	

126 TITLE:

WHEN THIS REVELATION WAS GIVEN:	WHERE THIS REVELATION WAS GIVEN:	WHAT WAS HAPPENING WHEN THIS REVELATION WAS GIVEN:
WHEN	WHERE	WHY

What important doctrines and principles do you learn from this section (use the footnotes)?

_____

_____

_____

_____

_____

_____

_____

_____

_____

_____

_____

_____

_____

TITLE:

	WHEN THIS REVELATION WAS GIVEN:	WHERE THIS REVELATION WAS GIVEN:	WHAT WAS HAPPENING WHEN THIS REVELATION WAS GIVEN:
WHEN		WHERE	Sections 127 and 128 are both letters from Joseph to the Saints concerning baptism for the dead.

VERSES	WHAT IS HAPPENING, DOCTRINES & PRINCIPLES TAUGHT	WORDS LOOKED UP	INSIGHTS GAINED & LESSONS LEARNED
127:1-2			
127:3-4			
127:5-9			
127:10-12			
128:1-4			
128:5-8			
128:9-12			
128:13-15			
128:16-18			
128:19-20			
128:21-22			
128:23-25			

DOCTRINE & COVENANTS 129-130

129 TITLE:

WHEN	WHEN THIS REVELATION WAS GIVEN:	WHERE	WHERE THIS REVELATION WAS GIVEN:	WHY	WHAT WAS HAPPENING WHEN THIS REVELATION WAS GIVEN:
					Many Saints were curious about angels, spirits and resurrected persons. This revelation distinguishes how to identify various messengers.

Study this section. As you study the verses below, record all of the doctrines and principles you can find in each verse's box. Include obvious ones and not-so-obvious doctrines and principles.

1-3 Two kinds of beings in heaven	4-8 How to identify different types of angels	9 3 grand keys

130 TITLE:

WHEN	WHEN THIS REVELATION WAS GIVEN:	WHERE	WHERE THIS REVELATION WAS GIVEN:	WHY	WHAT WAS HAPPENING WHEN THIS REVELATION WAS GIVEN:

Study this section. As you study the verses below, record all of the doctrines and principles you can find in each verse's box. Include obvious ones and not-so-obvious doctrines and principles.

1-3 Heavenly Father and Christ appear personally to men	4-7 Where angels reside	8-9 The celestial earth	10-11 A white stone

12-17 Time of Second Coming	18-19 The importance of gaining intelligence	20-21 Blessings come by obedience to law	22-23 The Father and Son have bodies

THE FATHER AND SON HAVE BODIES
OF FLESH AND BONE

22 The Father has a body of flesh and bones as tangible as man's; the Son also; but the Holy Ghost has not a body of flesh and bones, but is a personage of Spirit. Were it not so, the Holy Ghost could not dwell in us.

23 A man may receive the Holy Ghost, and it may descend upon him and not tarry with him.

DOCTRINE & COVENANTS 130:22-23

"If any of us could now see the God we are striving to serve – if we could see our Father who dwells in the Heavens, we should learn that we are as well acquainted with him as we are with our earthly father, and he would be as familiar to us in the expression of his countenance and we should be ready to embrace him and fall upon his neck and kiss him, if we had the privilege. And still we, unless the vision of the Spirit is opened to us, know nothing about God. You know much about him, if you but realize it. And there is no other one item that will so astound you, when your eyes are opened in eternity, as to think that you were so stupid in the body."

BRIGHAM YOUNG
Journal of Discourses 8:30

1. What doctrines (truths) and principles can you find in these verses?

2. Why do you think it is important to understand that Heavenly Father and Jesus Christ are separate individuals with bodies of flesh and bones?

3. Other religions do not have this understanding. In the year A.D. 325, the Christian world was disagreeing on the nature of God. Constantine (who was the emperor of Rome at the time) gathered the religious leaders and had them state their beliefs. It grew into a heated debate and in the end they voted on what the nature of God was. A creed (statement of belief) was written, and that creed was called the Nicene Creed. That Creed's basic elements are still part of Christianity today and it states that Heavenly Father, Jesus Christ, and the Holy Ghost are the same personage rather than three separate beings. It teaches that there are three ways to be God, but they are all part of one God (which is a spirit / essence, not a man).

   - What do you find wrong with the above method of discovering the nature of God?

   - The truths from the Nicene Creed were what Joseph Smith was taught in the churches he attended. What did he learn in an instant during the First Vision that restored the truth of the nature of God?

   - How does understanding the nature of Heavenly Father impact your relationship with Him?

   - How does understanding the nature of Heavenly Father help you understand who YOU are?

. What do these scriptures teach you about the seminary doctrinal topic: "The Godhead"?

DOCTRINE & COVENANTS 131 TITLE:

	WHEN THIS REVELATION WAS GIVEN:		WHERE THIS REVELATION WAS GIVEN:		WHAT WAS HAPPENING WHEN THIS REVELATION WAS GIVEN:
WHEN		WHERE		WHY	

VERSES	DOCTRINES AND PRINCIPLES TAUGHT	WORDS LOOKED UP	THOUGHTS, INSIGHTS, & LESSONS LEARNED
1			
2			
3			
4			
5			
6			
7			
8			

DOCTRINE & COVENANTS 131:1-4

THE NEW AND EVERLASTING COVENANT OF MARRIAGE

1 In the celestial glory there are three heavens or degrees;

2 And in order to obtain the highest, a man must enter into this order of the priesthood [meaning the new and everlasting covenant of marriage];

3 And if he does not, he cannot obtain it.

4 He may enter into the other, but that is the end of his kingdom; he cannot have an increase.

DOCTRINE & COVENANTS 131:1-4

"Two compelling doctrinal reasons help us to understand why eternal marriage is essential to the Father's plan.

"Reason 1: The natures of male and female spirits complete and perfect each other, and therefore men and women are intended to progress together toward exaltation. ...

"By divine design, men and women are intended to progress together toward perfection and a fulness of glory. Because of their distinctive temperaments and capacities, males and females each bring to a marriage relationship unique perspectives and experiences. The man and the woman contribute differently but equally to a oneness and a unity that can be achieved in no other way. The man completes and perfects the woman and the woman completes and perfects the man as they learn from and mutually strengthen and bless each other. ...

"Reason 2: By divine design, both a man and a woman are needed to bring children into mortality and to provide the best setting for the rearing and nurturing of children" (*"Marriage Is Essential to His Eternal Plan,"*

ELDER DAVID A. BEDNAR
Ensign, June 2006, 83–84

1. What did Joseph Smith reveal about the Celestial Kingdom in verse 1?

2. What do we need to do to obtain the highest degree of the Celestial Kingdom (verses 2-4)?

3. What do you think it means in verse 4 that if we are not sealed in the temple by the proper authority, we "cannot have an increase"?

4. According to Elder Bednar (in the quote above), why is marriage between a man and a woman necessary for our exaltation?

5. How could understanding the doctrine that celestial marriage is essential for exaltation affect what you look for in a future spouse?

6. Why is it important at your age to make it a priority to prepare to be married eternally in the temple?

7. What can you do to prepare yourself to have a marriage worthy of the highest degree of the Celestial Kingdom?

8. What do these scriptures teach you about the seminary doctrinal topic: "Marriage and Family"?

DOCTRINE & COVENANTS 132 TITLE:

WHEN THIS REVELATION WAS GIVEN:	WHERE THIS REVELATION WAS GIVEN:	WHAT WAS HAPPENING WHEN THIS REVELATION WAS GIVEN:
WHEN	WHERE	WHY

1-3 If revealed, must obey	**4-6** The new and everlasting covenant	**7** The conditions of this law	**8-14** Must come by His law
15-18 Marriage in the world	**19-20** Marriage by His law	**21-25** The strait and narrow way	**26-27** Consequences of sins
28-33 Abrahamic Covenant	**34-40** Joseph restored promises made in ages before	**41-44** Consequences of adultery	**45-47** Joseph has power to bind and seal
48-50 Joseph sealed to exaltation	**51-57** Counsel to Emma Smith	**58-62** Law of plural wives	**63-66** Law of plural wives

TITLE:

WHEN THIS REVELATION WAS GIVEN:	WHERE THIS REVELATION WAS GIVEN:	WHAT WAS HAPPENING WHEN THIS REVELATION WAS GIVEN:
WHEN	WHERE	WHY

1-6 Prepare for the Second Coming	**7-9** Go forth to Zion	**10-16** Go ye out from Babylon	**17-24** The Lord will stand on Mount Zion
25-30 Lost tribes will come forth	**31-35** Tribe of Judah shall be sanctified	**36-40** The gospel was restored to preach to the world	**41-45** The Lord will bring punishment to the world
46-49 When Christ appears	**50-51** And His voice shall be heard	**52-55** The year of the redeemed is come	**56** The graves shall be opened
57-59 The Gospel sent forth in plainness	**60-63** For this cause the commandments were given	**64-70** The destruction that will come	**71-74** The destruction that will come

DOCTRINE & COVENANTS 134 TITLE:

WHEN	WHEN THIS REVELATION WAS GIVEN:	WHERE	WHERE THIS REVELATION WAS GIVEN:	WHY	WHAT WAS HAPPENING WHEN THIS REVELATION WAS GIVEN:

VERSES	DOCTRINES AND PRINCIPLES TAUGHT	WORDS LOOKED UP	THOUGHTS, INSIGHTS, & LESSONS LEARNED
1-2			
3-4			
5			
6			
7-8			
9-10			
11			
12			

WHEN	WHEN THIS REVELATION WAS GIVEN:	WHERE	WHERE THIS REVELATION WAS GIVEN:	WHY	WHAT WAS HAPPENING WHEN THIS REVELATION WAS GIVEN:

	What I learned about the martyrdom of Joseph and Hyrum Smith	What lessons can I learn from these verses?
When, where, who, and how verse 1		
The others in the room verse 2		
What Joseph Smith accomplished verse 3		
On their way to Carthage verse 4		
Ether 12:36-38 verse 5		
The best blood of the nineteenth century verse 6		
Their innocent blood verse 7		

JOSEPH SMITH LABORED FOR OUR SALVATION

Joseph Smith, the Prophet and Seer of the Lord, has done more, save Jesus only, for the salvation of men in this world, than any other man that ever lived in it. In the short space of twenty years, he has brought forth the Book of Mormon, which he translated by the gift and power of God, and has been the means of publishing it on two continents; has sent the fulness of the everlasting gospel, which it contained, to the four quarters of the earth; has brought forth the revelations and command- ments which compose this book of Doctrine and Covenants, and many other wise documents and instructions for the benefit of the children of men; gathered many thousands of the Latter-day Saints, founded a great city, and left a fame and name that cannot be slain. He lived great, and he died great in the eyes of God and his people; and like most of the Lord's anointed in ancient times, has sealed his mission and his works with his own blood; and so has his brother Hyrum. In life they were not divided, and in death they were not separated!

"To questions about Joseph's character, we might share the words of thousands who knew him personally and who gave their lives for the work he helped establish. John Taylor, who was shot four times by the mob that killed Joseph, would later declare: 'I testify before God, angels, and men, that [Joseph] was a good, honorable, [and] virtuous man— ... [and] that his private and public character was unim- peachable—and that he lived and died as a man of God.'"

ELDER NEIL L. ANDERSEN
October 2014 General Conference

DOCTRINE & COVENANTS 135:3

1. This scripture was part of the announcement of the martyrdom and was included in the Doctrine and Covenants. Make a list of everything this scripture teaches that Joseph Smith accomplished in his lifetime:

2. What is a line in this scripture that is the most touching to you? Why?

3. What does this scripture teach you about the seminary doctrinal topic: "The Restoration"?

WHEN	WHEN THIS REVELATION WAS GIVEN:	WHERE	WHERE THIS REVELATION WAS GIVEN:	WHY	WHAT WAS HAPPENING WHEN THIS REVELATION WAS GIVEN:

VERSES	INSTRUCTIONS GIVEN TO CAMP OF ISRAEL
1-3	
4-7	
8-11	
12-15	
16-18	
19-21	
22-26	
27-29	
30-32	
33-35	
36-37	
38-39	
40-42	

DOCTRINE & COVENANTS 137 TITLE:

WHEN	WHEN THIS REVELATION WAS GIVEN:	WHERE	WHERE THIS REVELATION WAS GIVEN:	WHY	WHAT WAS HAPPENING WHEN THIS REVELATION WAS GIVEN:

VERSES	DOCTRINES AND PRINCIPLES TAUGHT	WORDS LOOKED UP	THOUGHTS, INSIGHTS, & LESSONS LEARNED
1-2			
3-4			
5			
6			
7			
8			
9			
10			

TITLE:

	WHEN THIS REVELATION WAS GIVEN:	WHERE THIS REVELATION WAS GIVEN:		WHAT WAS HAPPENING WHEN THIS REVELATION WAS GIVEN:
WHEN		**WHERE**	**WHY**	

VERSES	DOCTRINES, INSTRUCTIONS, AND PRINCIPLES TAUGHT	WORDS LOOKED UP	INSIGHTS, THOUGHTS, & LESSONS LEARNED
1-2			
3-4			
5-10			
11			
12-13			
14-15			
16-17			
18-19			
20-21			
22-23			
24-25			
26-27			

VERSES	DOCTRINES AND PRINCIPLES TAUGHT	WORDS LOOKED UP	INSIGHTS, THOUGHTS, & LESSONS LEARNED
28-29		155	
30			
31-32			
33-34			
35-37			
38-41			
42-46			
47-49			
50			
51-52			
53-54			
55-56			
57			
58-60			